Modern Macramé Book for Beginners and Beyond

Stylish Modern Macramé Design Patterns and Project Ideas for Plant Hangers, Wall Hangings, and More for Your Home Décor…With Illustrations

By

Alice Green

Copyright © 2020 – Alice Green

All rights reserved

No part of this publication may be reproduced, distributed, or transmitted in any form or by any means, including photocopying, recording, or other electronic or mechanical methods, without the prior written permission of the publisher, except in the case of brief quotations embodied in reviews and certain other non-commercial uses permitted by copyright law.

Disclaimer

This publication is designed to provide competent and reliable information regarding the subject matter covered. However, the views expressed in this publication are those of the author alone, and should not be taken as expert instruction or professional advice. The reader is responsible for his or her own actions.

The author hereby disclaims any responsibility or liability whatsoever that is incurred from the use or application of the contents of this publication by the purchaser or reader. The purchaser or reader is hereby responsible for his or her own actions.

Table of Contents

Introduction 6

Chapter 1 8

What is Macramé? 8

    A Short Trip Down Memory Lane 9

    Every Day Uses of Macramé... 13

    Health Benefits of Macramé.. 20

    Macramé Knots and Patterns.. 23

        Lark's Head Knot 23
        Square Knots 25
        Hitch Knot 33
        Spiral Knot.. 37
        Wind Knot 39

Chapter 2 40

Basic Macramé Terms 40

Chapter 3 47

Tips and Tricks for Neat Macramé Knotting 47

Chapter 4 60

Getting Started with Macramé 60

Essential Materials and Tools Needed 60
    Cord/Rope 60
    Beads 67
    Wood or Dowels 73
    Adhesive Tapes 80
    Scissors 85
    Pliers 86
    Knotting Boards 89
    Metal Ring or Hoops 90
    Measuring Tape 91
    Tape 91

Chapter 5 92

Macramé Projects for Home Decoration 92

    Macramé Hanging Chair 92

    Brass Ring Macramé Dream Catcher 97

    Macramé Wall Hanging 107

    Macramé Room Divider 116

    Macramé Mirror Wall Hanger 126

    Easy Macramé Plant Hanger 132

    Macramé Table Runners 137

Chapter 6 149

Other Macramé Project Designs 149

    Openwork Macramé Bracelets 149

    Dyed Macramé Necklace 164

    Easy Macramé Earrings... 168

Chapter 7 178

Frequently Asked Questions (FAQs) 178

Introduction

There has been a long age tradition of using knots to create various forms of textile and artistry pieces. This technique makes use of special procedures to achieve its goal. Over the years, artists have found a way of reinventing this long age trade.

Macramé is a practice that has lasted for thousands of years. The textile industry has held on to this form of art for a pretty long time. As the world evolved, there also arose a need to scale the degree of macramé to a large extent so that it can still find application in today's world and remain relevant. Many innovations have started taking the idea of macramé beyond just plant and wall hangers. Macramé can likewise be used to produce, among many other things, like key chains and table runners.

In this book, you will be enlightened on how to make some of the most eye-popping macramé designs with step-by-step graphical illustrations to compliment your read. Whatever the reason may be for which you want to learn macramé knotting, whether for the beauty of the art, for commercial profits or even for recreational purposes, this book is your best tool to achieving your goal.

Through the in-depth illustrations discussed in this book, you'll soon learn to make your first macramé knot in no time. There are also some advanced level macramé designs for you in this book should you decide you are fit enough to go beyond the basics.

Chapter 1

What is Macramé?

Macramé are simply textiles or textile materials produced through knotting. There are several types of knots that could be used to create a macramé and they run from basic to more complex ones. Asides the fact that commercial industries would require equipment like the mounting rings, you can use your hands to achieve the knots. It is as simple to produce like that. You can venture into it while you sit idle at home or probably bored at work. To call something macramé, it has to have a basic form of a knot. However, some macramé materials involve other techniques like weaving and knitting.

A more popular form of the macramé design would be the "reef knot" or what we rather call a square macramé, hitches and half hitches. These ones were created by sailors who needed to produce ornamental knots that could be worn and used to design interior spaces. They also needed it to cover their knives, bottles and ship parts. Macramé techniques are used to also create leather belts and other forms of fabric.

Today, macramé can be used to design bracelets, jewelry and decoration materials. Macramé began gaining ground in the 1970s. You can imagine how long this art has lasted for. It joins other ancient crafts like embroidery, quilting and needlework. Amongst all these, macramé seems to be the only form of artwork presently experiencing a revamp.

Macramé not only makes use of plant fibers like cotton and wool, although they might be the popular ones you see, glasses, dyed threads can also be added to give it a more stylish and impressive look.

A Short Trip Down Memory Lane

Macramé has always been an ancient tradition that dates far back into the middle ages. To appreciate this artistic invention, we need to take a look at history to understand where it originated and the people who made it more popular in the modern-day.

In the early 1970's we can acknowledge that lots of tapestries, hangers and accessories were found at almost every house and building. These were all seen to have been made through knotted designs. The evolution of macramé art has been attributed to the

Arabians. The word macramé originated from the Arabic word migramah also called fringe. History records the Arabian weavers as the first to use knots to create beautiful pieces as far back as the thirteenth century. These knots were placed on the lining of towels and shawls. Their decorative knots were also used to finish handwoven textiles. At that time, there was no machinery and equipment which could handle weaving and knotting, and so they decided to make use of their hands. Macramé is also believed to have come from the Turkish word makrama, which is used to describe towels and napkins styled with knots. We can also trace it back to China in its third-century reign, where ancient palaces used macramé to produce special textiles and wall hangings placed in palaces. It was quite a beauty to behold.

It is not precisely sure where the macramé technique came from because it would be a lot difficult to have a specific location as the initial place where macramé production started. This is so because there were not a lot of records and documentation procedures in place but what we are certain is the period when these innovations began, the thirteenth century.

As soon as Arabic artists showcased their artistry, it continued to spread to other parts of the world, starting from Europe. Sailors also have a part to contribute to the story being told about macramé. In fact, we can say that sustaining macramé into the modern age was possible because sailors had a role to play in it. It would have vanished into thin air as other artistry pieces have. Knots had many applications in ships and this was why the demand and supply of macramé doubled because they needed it for various furnishings.

When they got to some new towns and bays, they would sell it to persons who loved the design. At other times, it was used as exchanges for food, clothing and the rest. The Victorian era saw macramé being used as decorations to clothes and textiles, which by now, many more had learned the skill of production. This was why it was easier incorporating it into the fashion world. It was also during this period that macramé became old and obsolete.

Macramé began to fade gradually in the 1900s, though it didn't vanish totally, it was limited to being traded as a commodity for less than half of the European and American continent. The boom came back around the 1970s. It could be seen as a sheer coincidence that macramé happened to have received a boom at the time when feminists were in the early stages of their agitation. It was during this period when women began to take active participation in the craft. This further acted as a spur of gender wars and inequality as women sought to take the trade above the reach of their male counterparts. These women were already suffering from the abuse faced in marriage, motherhood and the struggle of financial and sexual freedom. They used their spare time to perfect the art. Their approach, however, was a bit wild, untamed and uninhibited. This era saw virtually unlimited usage for macramé designs.

It is being believed that a set of moors got to familiarize the knot tying patterns. This introduction lasted until the fifteenth century, where it was eventually spread to the French and Italian regions. It was in the seventeenth century that the Queen of England opted to teach ladies who were kept on waiting how they could make macramé. A certain queen called Queen Victoria, whose name was used to mark the Victorian era made the form of art more exposed and widespread throughout all the lands even as women took particular interests.

We have seen that in present times, women have become anchors of this trend. This was not so when it first began. Most of the best producers of macramé were men. These men were mostly sailors who had understood the importance of knots, especially the square knot. They already knew that knots could be used to secure ships, load cargos making use of ropes and ensure safety while sailing. Knot tying was an ancient practice already employed to ease the stress sailors had to go through, especially when sailing. The more they spent time on the sea, the more they needed to strengthen the knots used to hold the ship and direct movement. They discovered these knots could also be used to uphold bells and rope ladders. With the ease of obtaining materials used for making macramé, they found their leisure time yielding many profits.

Every Day Uses of Macramé

There are vast applications we can use macramé designs for when we talk about interior decorations. Macramé has been found to give and add a stylish and befitting look to your homes, offices and halls. As a result of the number of combinations that could be achieved with it, it is a perfect option for hanging, covering and keeping items. It can be designed in such a way that it fits other items and objects. If you're looking out for a new touch around your shopping arena or want to give your home a great taste of class and beauty, macramé is one reliable option for you. Here we have set out to enumerate a few common ways macramé can be used today.

Macramé Tapestry

Mounting a macramé tapestry in your home will surely add class and beauty to your home. When you look at the sections of your house and walls which look dull and uninteresting, tapestry is a good option to change the description you see. These designs could also be hanged above the headboard of beds and sofas both in the bedroom and sitting room. You could choose to attach the tapestry to a wooden and slender limb of a tree so that you can obtain a more natural and vegetative look to the eyes. This attachment could also prevent macramé tapestry design from sagging. Sagging means that it begins to lose its alignment and placement in the areas of the house where it has been arranged. It has been observed that macramé wall arts really bring out the aesthetic value of the craft.

Dream Cutchers

A dream catcher made as macramé is a very exquisite way of telling visitors so many things about the house and family where they have walked into. You can use this to make guests feel a lot welcome and heart warmed towards you. Some signals and messages you can pass across through this gesture include peace, restfulness, and positivity. Dream catchers are mostly made from iron wires. Instead of using such which gives no added design and feel, macramé dream catchers are better options. Macramé dream catchers are soft and tender such that they bring a diet of comfort and gentleness when you get close to them to touch. The fabrics and braids used in the production of such are well selected and woven together. Your dream catcher could be made more attractive and colorful when you also attach beads, feathers and some other decorative materials. You can engage in this simple but valuable craft so that you give your home an exquisite feel.

Macramé Curtains

You see, curtains are one element found in many homes. There is hardly a home you walk into that doesn't have a curtain or form of one located in one area of the house. From windows to doors to entrances and walkways, curtains are used to separate like parts of the house from another. Curtains can also be made to represent a decorative feature. The patterns and materials used for the manufacture of the curtain would tell how beautiful and aesthetic it becomes. There are varying degrees of weaves available to choose from. Some are dense while others are light and loosened to allow the entrance of light. The macramé curtains could also be rigged up to a runner such that whenever the curtain is to be opened, it is opened with so much ease.

Room Dividers

Room dividers can be made form macramé and are used to divide internal spaces. They are commonly made with noisy beads. The macramé dividers are designed to prevent and take care of the noises made from the rattling of the beads. If you choose to have your doors shut, you could attach the dividers to the frames of the doors so that the internal space is more or less open and inviting. The cords of the macramé room divider are laced with beads on strands so that there is a little weight even when they are disturbed to enable them to move into the original position. This is effective for covering entrances, ensuring a separation between rooms that exist very close to each other.

Lampshades

Most of the old designs we have in our homes are already looking unattractive and phased out. Macramé lamp stands come in handy at this point. Your dusty old lampshades can become beautiful and full of life by allowing it covered with macramé. Due to the ease with which the knots can be modified, we can successfully make them to different shades and sizes. You can customize the amount of light you want to be allowed through the lampstand. Some people go for something that allows a little amount of light, this they have achieved through denser and weightier weaving patterns. You can also go further by adding shells, beads and tassels to make the lampstands more complex and hard to decipher while still retaining the beauty it creates.

Furniture Covers

When you step into a lot of homes and offices, one thing you would agree to is that furniture is a must-have. They are one piece of materials you almost can't do without. Made and styled from woods of all taste and quality, you'll still need a macramé-made covering to make them more attractive. Whether they have already started getting old or not, getting them covered with macramé-made covers are a good way of maintaining their beauty. Even when you notice you have lost interest in having the furniture around, just wait and see how your love for them is rekindled with the introduction of macramé covers. This finishing makes your worn out and outdated stools and seat furniture a beauty to behold.

Pillows and Blankets

Pillows have become the word's largest sleeping material for many reasons. Some for medical reasons, probably from the need for the head to be kept in a particular position while sleeping. Others include comfort and ease with sleep. Some pillows are so beautifully designed that anytime you get to them, they invoke a feeling of rest. Some chair accessories can be made with macramé designed pillows so that when you rest on them, you feel relaxed and calm. Blankets come in handy when in need of company and when the weather temperature drops considerably. This drop in temperature will initiate the need for proper protection from the hazards of cold. When selecting fabrics to uses in the production of such, you more likely should make macramé your chosen desire if you are looking for the best experience with comfort.

Table Runner

There is a special effect and look macramé table runners attract to your dining spaces. Some dining spaces look so empty and boring with no form of art nor appeal to the eyes. These effects are what we refer to as negative spaces. These negative spaces can be broken with macramé runners. When visitors come into your spaces, the kind of table runner they are made to see can also be an invite that keeps them coming back all the time. It is much of a psychological effect you create in their minds. This is not just limited to home dining spaces; it also includes restaurants, eateries and fast foods. This would make your customers have more of a personalized experience. There are so many competitors bidding for the patronage of your customers. You can keep them still coming through the kind of service they are given. One effective way of ensuring this is to design your eating space with macramé table runners. Macramé runners could also be placed in gardens and living rooms to arrange flowers, candles and some centerpieces. Doing this doesn't take away the eating space, so why not choose this as a way of making your eating space more comfortable and heartwarming. You can go a little further by attaching a long fringe at both ends of the table runner. Another way you get to enjoy these macramé table runners are when you go out for spring vacations or hangouts with friends and family. They can create a bright touch and beauty, trust me. Macramé designs for table runners are more appreciated because individuals get to view them from a closer angle. The perception is different when the view is a little far since you sit close to it, you can easily observe the patterns and weave lines.

Textile Frames

Whether you want your mirror outlined or you want the frame you're currently using hidden, macramé frames are a good choice for you. You may be needing a contrast with the focal point on your frames; this can be achieved using macramé frames. You can be sure to avoid issues of trust and compatibility as it is well taken care of through customized designs. When we talk of frames, we are not just limiting it to residential use. These frames can also be used in offices, shops, halls and a lot of other areas.

Health Benefits of Macramé

It serves as a relaxation therapy

Stress therapy has been a major agitation in the world today. With the rise in so many activities and busy schedules of many, there is a need to bring balance through actions that calm the nerves and reduce tension. Depression and anxiety are other emotional problems that need serious attention. All these arise from the body's response to some events and casualties. Macramé art is am an effective way of managing such stress. The processes involved in creating a piece of macramé art takes your attention away from the stress and emotional imbalances your body faces and focuses them on the art of crafting. The joy of having to create something beautiful is a good way of taking off unnecessary stressors.

As you craft different forms of macramé art, it helps you meditate. This meditation brings about peace and calmness in your entire body. This is why many people who are macramé crafters are most times joyful and happy. As you create different materials, it indirectly affects the neurons that are secreted in your brain. So, even when the emotions you're feeling at that point is a depressing emotion, your brain can secret other hormones that trigger up happiness and joy within you. The more time you spend making macramé, the more your mood and state of mind changes for the better.

It boosts your mental capacity

For many people, macramé means different things. For some, the skill of creating something that appeals to the eyes is both mental and intellectual. Intellectual in the sense that the individual has to come up with a really good design that makes his works stand out. This process indirectly increases your brain power and cognitive reasoning. You can use it as a medium to awaken your critical reasoning power, especially when you feel you are gradually losing control over it as a result of pressures from the office or family. Today so many have been celebrated on account of the beautiful pieces of art they have created. Sometimes you might not have all the necessary material to finish your design. Your ability to improvise and make use of what you have can boost your thinking capacity. So many of the early crafters of macramé, like the sailors, didn't always have all the desired components to build something nice. They only got the opportunity when they arrived in some cities and docked at some bays. This didn't also stop them from creating better designs because they made use of the available materials.

It strengthens your arms

Tying macramé knots and patterns help strengthen your arms and muscles. For persons who have begun experiencing conditions that weaken their arms and muscles, macramé knot tying can be used to bring back their strength. As you continue tying and knotting, you will find yourself gently receiving relief from your pain and muscle contractions. You will also discover your joints becoming free and loose.

Macramé Knots and Patterns

Lark's Head Knot

This, by far, is the most common and simplest knots you can find in macramé designs. It is very rare and uncommon not to find this knot embedded in any finished macramé design. The lark's head knot can be used when attaching your cording to a ring dowel or handle in your macramé project or just when you're about to start. Let's delve straight into knowing how this knot is made.

You begin by folding the macramé cords you have into two. This will form a loop; this loop should be placed under the ring or dowel.

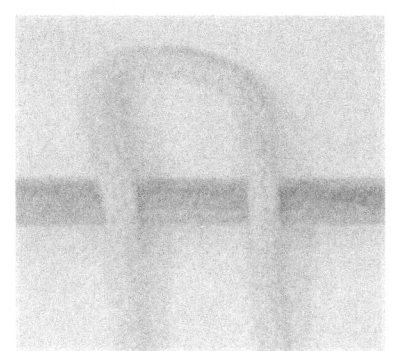

With the loop, try to fish out the ends of the cording. If you have done this successfully, you can pull tightly, creating your finished lark's knot.

Square Knots

This knot comprises of two lark's head knots. A square knot is one of the most widely used macramé knots, which can be created as either a left-facing half knot or right-facing half knot, depending on which side you start with.

Square knots need to have at least 4 cords (2 working cords and 2 filler cords). However, more can be accommodated. The working cords are the first and last cords. Let's call them working cord 1 and 4. The filler cords are the middle cords. Let's call them filler cord 2 and 3. These cords will switch places, but their original numbering will be maintained.

Left-Facing Square Knot

A left-facing square knot comes with a vertical bump that is visible on the left side of the finished knot.

Take the first cord on your left (working cord 1) and move it across the right side over the middle filler cords (2 and 3) and right under the last working cord (cord 4).

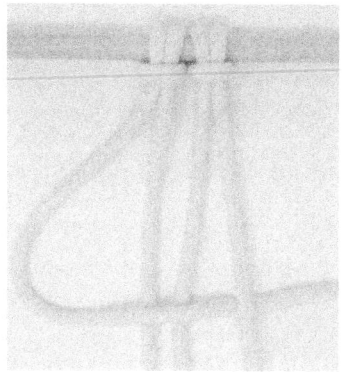

Take working cord 4 and move it across to the left, right under the two filler cords and over working cord 1.

Pull both cords 1 and 4 (working cords) to tighten, while keeping the filler cords straight. This is a left-facing half square knot.

Now, the working cords have swapped places with working cord 1 on the right and working cord 4 on the left. Take working cord 1 and move it across to the left, right across the two filler cords and right under working cord 4.

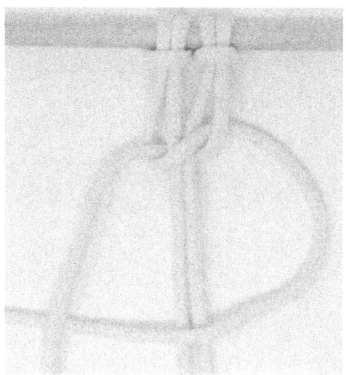

Take working cord 4 and move it across to the right, just under the two filler cords and over working cord 1.

Pull both working cords 1 and 4 to tighten, while keeping the filler cords straight. This completes your left-facing square knot.

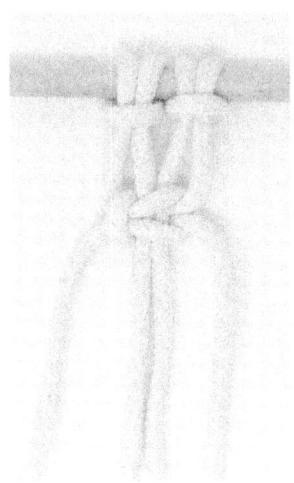

Right-Facing Square Knot

A right-facing square knot comes with a vertical bump that is visible on the right side of the finished knot.

Take the last cord on your right (working cord 4) and move it across the left side over the middle filler cords (2 and 3) and right under the first working cord (cord 1).

Take working cord 1 and move it across to the right, just under the two filler cords and over working cord 4.

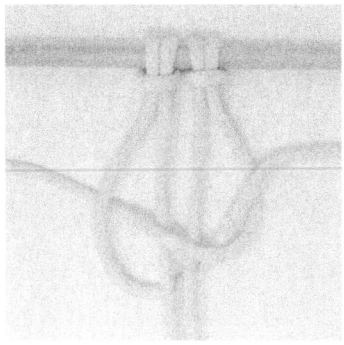

Pull both cords 1 and 4 (working cords) to tighten, while keeping the filler cords straight. This is a right-facing half square knot.

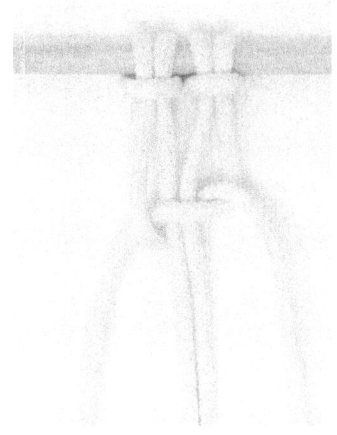

Now, the working cords have swapped places with working cord 1 on the right and working cord 4 on the left. Take working cord 4 and move it across to the right, just across the two filler cords and right under working cord 1.

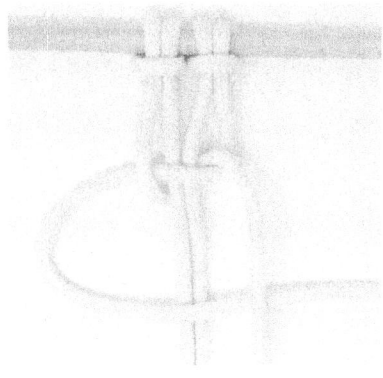

Take working cord 1 and move it across to the left, just under the two filler cords and over working cord 4.

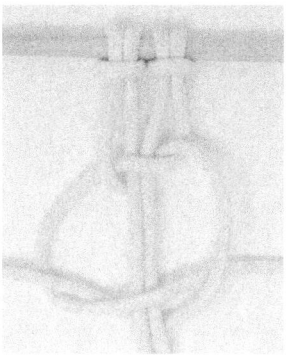

Pull both working cords 1 and 4 to tighten, while keeping the filler cords straight. This completes your right-facing square knot.

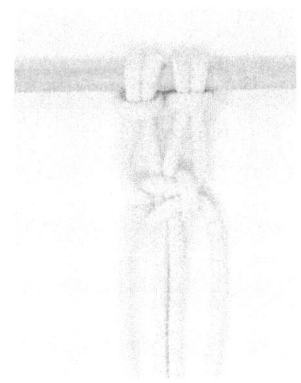

Hitch Knot

There are two forms of this knot, the half hitch and the double hitch. The hitch knot, like the lark's knot, is also a basic knot and doesn't require much process. When you make a hitch knot, you start by creating a lark's knot. When this is created, make one cord the fourth cord. Make sure the cord is looped through the fourth home and pull tightly. With this, you have a half hitch knot

Double Half Hitch

To create this, all you have to do is to create the half hitch twice. You can also create a diagonal pattern to the hitch knot. Here's how to make it:

You begin with three or more lark's head knots. If you use three mark head knots, you should have a total of six cords, while if you use four lark's head knots, you will have a total of eight cords. The following steps are implemented for three lark's head knots.

Take the outer left cord and place diagonally across the other five cords. This cord is your filler cord. The direction and the way you place the outer cord will determine the pattern you come out with. You need to ensure that the placement over the cords is appropriate to give you the desired results.

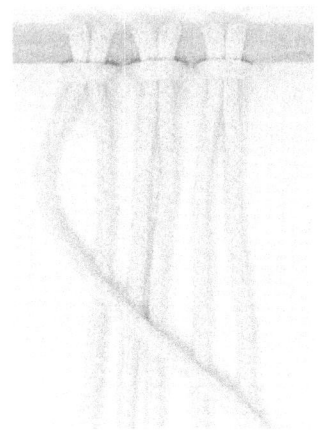

From your left to the right, you create a double half hitch knot using the second cord. Pull tightly and make sure that the outer left cord is still placed diagonally over the other cords.

Make a double half hitch knot with the third cord and another double half hitch with the fourth cord. You will keep on repeating this process until you get to the last cord on the right side. As you do this, a diagonal pattern will emerge.

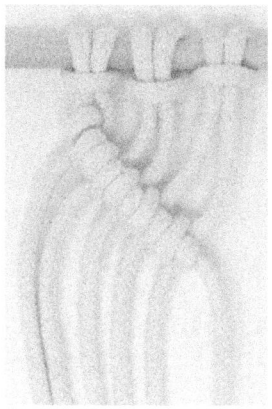

You need to repeat the entire process this time, beginning from right to left. Your outer right cord should be the one placed diagonally over the other cords.

Instead of making a diagonal line with the double half knots, you can choose to make them horizontally by placing the first cord horizontally.

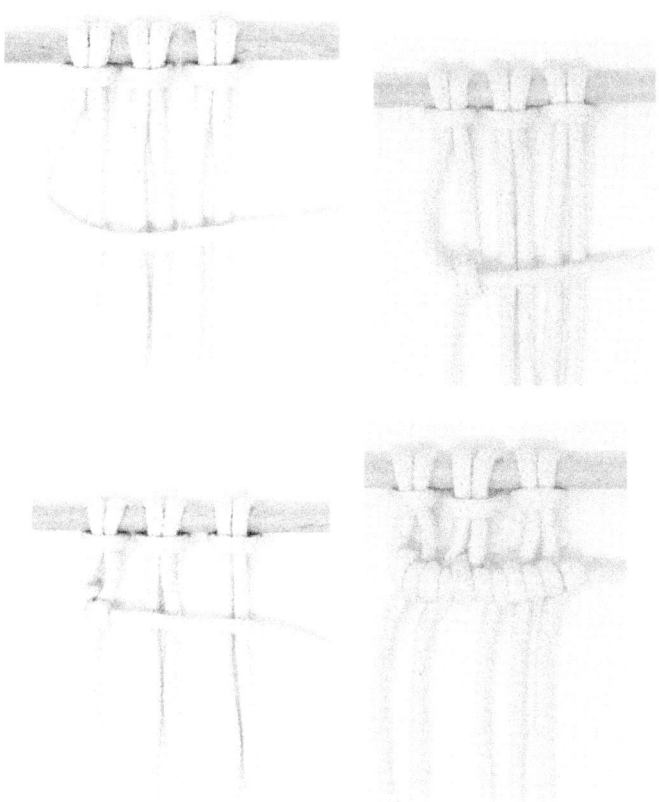

There are so many ways you can use the hitch knot. You can even use them to make triple half hitch knots. Hitch knots are a great choice for making amazing patterns.

Spiral Knot

Spiral knot falls into the category of pretty and easy knots. It is made by combining patterns of half-square knots or half hitch knots. When switching, you move from the right to the left side to complete the square knot.

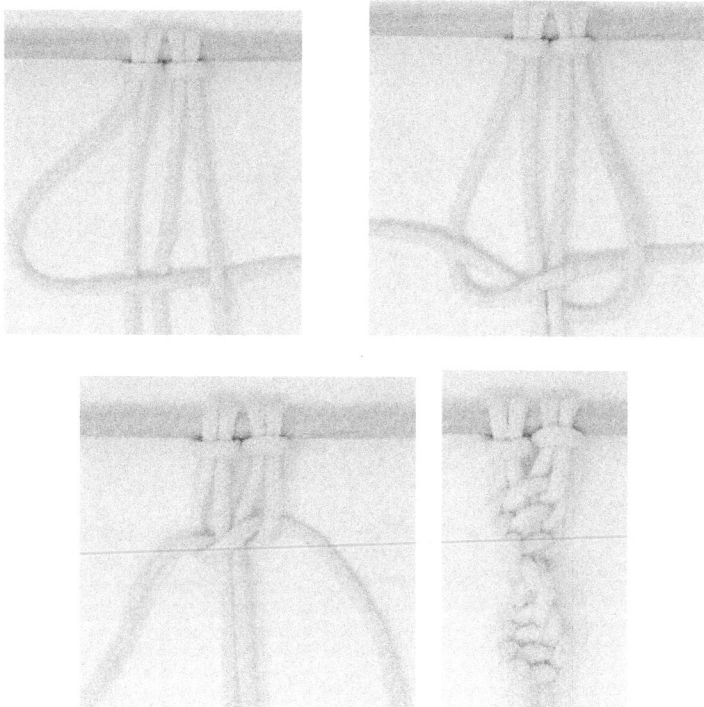

As you do this, the spiral will begin forming. If you need the spiral knot in thicker sizes, it is more advisable to begin with two lark's head knots. Single designs of the spiral knot are made with just one lark's head knot while repeating the half hitch knot patterns. As you do this, you will experience a twist.

Wind Knot

This type of knot is used for gathering many threads together, especially when you are about to end your work. To do this, you place extra amounts of threads above the cords. Wind the longest cord around other cords and pull. The end should be pulled through the loop of additional threads. When this thread is drawn down, you can choose to hide the short ends of your tassel.

Chapter 2

Basic Macramé Terms

Alternating cord: Forming a new set of cords by taking half of the cords from the adjacent knots that were previously tied and then tying a new knot, laying below and between where the cords originated.

ASK: This is an abbreviation for alternating square knot.

Band: This is a length of macramé that is wide and flat.

Bar: A bar is a series of knot which forms a raised area in a design. Bars can be created with half hitch knots and run horizontally, vertically or diagonally across a piece of macramé artwork.

Bight: A bight is a narrow section of a cord that is folded. It is mostly pushed through other parts of a knot.

Body: This is the main section of the project or design you are working on.

Braid: This can also be called a plait. It is created by crossing 3-4 cords such that they weave themselves around each other.

Braided cord: A braided cord is made up of several thin pieces of cords that have been woven together. Braided cords are studier than twisted cords.

Bundles: These are groups of cords that are gathered together

Button knot: A button knot is a knot which is round and tight

BH: This is an abbreviated form of a buttonhole. It is created by using vertical larks to produce loops used to fasten and join pieces.

Chinese macramé: These are knotted designs that originated in China and other Asian countries.

Crown knot: This is a decorative knot, also known as Shamrock Knot or the Chinese flower since it looks like a flower when finished.

Combination knot: this is achieved through the combination of two knots that form a new knot or design.

Cord – Cord is any material or fiber used to create macramé projects

Core – Any cord which runs through the center of the project while still knotted around it is called a core. They can also be fillers or central cords.

Crook – The curved section of a loop of cord.

Diagonal – This refers to a row of knots that run from the upper left to the lower right or in a reversed manner. Diagonal knots are mostly used with half hitch knots in macramé designs.

Diameter: This refers to the width of a cord measured in millimeters.

DDH – Double half hitch. This term is used to signify two half hitch knots created side by side.

Fillers – These cords usually stay at the center of a design or piece of macramé construction. They are knotted around the center of the design. They could be also be called core cords.

Findings – These are more of a fastening than actual cords. Their function in the design is to create closures, attachments and other elements that can serve as decorations. Examples of items used as findings are ear wires and clasps.

Finishing knot – This knot is tied to secure ends of a cord to prevent them from being unraveled.

Fringe –These are the length of cord ends that are knitted but left hanging

Fusion knots –This is another term used to denote combination knots.

Gusset – This is used when designing 3D projects such as bags and hangers.

Hitch –A hitch is a knot used to attach cords to other items.

Horizontal design – This is used to connote a design made from one side to another

Interlace – An interlace is a pattern where cords are mixed to create links between various areas of the design.

Inverted – Upside down.

Knotting cord –These are cords used to tie together knots used in a design.

Loop – This is a circular or oval-shaped space formed when two parts of a cord are passed over each other.

Micro-Macramé – Any macramé project or design made with small diameter materials can be called a micro macramé. The materials used mostly fall within the range of two diameters.

Mount – These are materials in the form of rings or frames which are used as part of the macramé design. You may also decide to use wooden handles to hang your cords when you begin designing. The wooden handles serve as your mount.

Natural –This is used to refer to cords and materials made from plants, wood or any form of natural source, which can include hemps and cottons.

Netting – Any pattern of knots which at the end will have open spaces in between is a net. This pattern can be used to create bags and hangers.

OH – This is an abbreviation, which means Overhand Knot.

Picot – These are loops formed at the beginning of the design. You will see them more when the design is still in its early phases.

Scallops – These are loops of knots created at the edges of macramé designs.

Segment – A segment can be a specific area of a cord, knot or design.

Sennit – This term refers to identical knots tied in a chain-like manner from one to another; some call it sinnets.

Standing end – This is the end of a cord that has been secured by a macramé board or any other surface which isn't used in the construction of the knot.

SK (Square Knot): This knot is very common and is created by tying 2 cords over other cords. These cords can either be single or multiple.

Stitch – This is used at the early crafting stages of a knot to replace it until it has been fully knotted

Synthetic – These are fibers made from chemical processes, which include polypropylene and nylon.

Vintage – These patterns have lasted for a long period of time, as far back as the 1900s. A large number of them are still in use today without a significant change to the knotting technique even as others continue to fall into extinction.

Weave – To weave is to make a cord placed so well that they can pass beneath each other without any restriction.

Chapter 3

Tips and Tricks for Neat Macramé Knotting

Are you getting fed up with the frustration that comes with designing macramé projects?

Sometimes being creative might not be the only factor responsible for the difficulties encountered while trying to learn and execute macramé designs. This is why this book has taken out time to give valuable tips that can help you through difficult times. For a long time, the act of crafting macramé pieces has stood as a mystery and a difficult task to handle. So many have been discouraged by the efforts needed to master the skill.

When creating macramé designs, your knots and finishes need to evoke an aesthetic appeal to your viewers. Though it also needs to be able to handle the purpose for which it was designed, e.g., a macramé plant hanger must be well crafted to be able to hold the plants in it without falling off. The same goes for other forms of hangers, chains, and various macramé designs.

As you deliberately pay attention to the tips you'll be shown subsequently, you will successfully overcome the creative blocks involved in macramé knots.

As a beginner with macramé designs, there are some essential tips that would help you achieve better results. Macramé is one form of art that has no specified rule. This makes it very complicated, especially when you begin making different patterns and knots. This frustration has made many opt out of the design process. It is important that we help you with some of this relevant information so that you can break past the limitations that you might be faced with.

Start with basic Knots

At first, it may seem that there are different knots that appear confusing and look difficult to handle. As you progress, you will get used to a variety of patterns and knots which would add beauty to your design. You should try as much as possible to get used to the square knot. It is among the basic knots you should be used to and a very good place to grow expertise in as a beginner. It should be your most trusted and used knot even as you try to incorporate others.

Attend trainings and seminars

As much as learning can be done individually, there are some areas of crafting you can't be able to achieve unless showed by an expert or someone with solid knowledge. When you attend trainings, you get connected to others with like minds and even others experiencing challenges like you do. This exposure has its way of spurring you up to better achievements. You can even make some friends and acquaintances who you'll run to for help when you encounter any difficulties while designing your macramé. At trainings, you'll be introduced to modern designs and easier ways of achieving better results.

Learn online

As the world continues to evolve, so technology continues to evolve. This has fostered the introduction of tons of information on the Internet. The internet has become a global village where you can get various information on various subject matters. When you surf the internet, you come across relevant information about macramé and other techniques that are available. Learning has gone past physical meetings and coordinated trainings. You can hop on to virtual learning platforms where there are visual aids to make you understand what you are doing much better. You get to see the person twist his hands, perform the loop and so on. You can even get books online embedded with step by step pictures on how you can perform a series of knots. As you follow them, you experience the ease with which these designs are created.

The resources available to you can either be free or paid. Whatever the means, ensure that you are updated on modern trends and techniques. Don't assume that the information you have at your disposal is good enough. Desire to know more.

Being expressive with your art

The mistake most people make is that they want to be so uptight with their designs so that they don't miss out on already set standards. The truth is that no matter how well you tend to imitate others and follow their guidance, you will always have your unique area of strength. Don't be afraid of making mistakes. A lot of mistakes are what have propelled so many of the world's greatest inventions. Your mistake might be a classic masterpiece for someone else. It all depends on how you view it. Allow your creativity to guide you into the best designs. Even though some persons do it for fun of having to create macramé materials, others do it as a source of daily income. People will only pay you according to the beauty they see when they look at your design. Don't hold back yourself and don't be too hard on yourself either.

Be patient

Give yourself time to get used to the art, continue experimenting with the various patterns you have learned and keep on developing your macramé knot skills. When learning, try infusing your own ideas into the design; it makes you discover things faster. Patiently correct mistakes you notice and don't give up on yourself. Some times, learning a particular knot or pattern may take you days and even sleepless nights, don't allow it to deter you from pushing on. Eventually, you'll get it if you don't give up. Most of the time, you'll find yourself correcting mistakes and revisiting old designs before proceeding to better ones.

This is why you need to have mastered basic knots like the square knot before moving on to other knots. Your mastery over the basic ones will help you smoothly get adjusted to more complex ones. As you learn these new knots, practice them more on clipboards. Don't take new ideas and patterns to a client's job or one you intend to use for a serious purpose. If you do this, you might end up ruining the entire material. Whatever you want to implement on your project should be something you're very sure you can handle. You should also be patient enough to take along with you a good pair of scissors with which you trim excesses from ropes. When you allow them to accumulate without trimming, it becomes more difficult to cut out. A sturdy comb can be helpful when brushing out clusters or fingers of cords and knots.

Binder clips

As a beginner, you will find these very helpful and efficient with the crafting of knots. It is much easier working with ropes suspended from the doors and frames. You can do this with nails and hooks. Some knots require that you suspend them because of their length, so it's wise for you to do so using clips so that they don't get entangled together and cause you more problems.

Take, for instance, while learning the square knot, you can clip the middle lengths of the cords to a board (either cutting or chipboard). In doing this, you won't have to worry about the tension while working with lengths to create knots.

You should also remember to cut more cord lengths than you feel you'll be needing. As you progress, you'll find out that your accuracy and precision with measurement will become better. At first, it isn't safe to rely on your intuition on what lengths to take. So many times, when you think the length and number you're using is okay, you will be disappointed. Since excesses can be trimmed and used for other tassels so that it doesn't turn out a waste, cutting more cord lengths is the best way to go as a beginner.

A good way of determining lengths would be to measure the length you need for your project and multiply it by four. This length will enable you to cut the cord to an appropriate length. The length method proposed is just for cutting ropes and not cords. Running out of cords and attaching new ones can slow down your progress and even obstruct the flow of your design. You can encounter entangling issues where you have to cut and redesign your entire project.

Avoiding stress

You know many eager folks want to do so much within the limits of their knowledge and experience. This makes them avoid breaks and relaxation periods. They feel it affects their workflow. The truth is that there is a limit to which you can stretch your body system. You can't be tough on your muscles to avoid them from relaxing. Macramé crafting takes lots of energy and can be very draining at times.

The kind of workstation you use can also be a contributing factor to the stress you will experience. There is no strict rule on what kind of workstation to use. Just find something comfortable enough. It might be on the floor, sofa, or even while standing. Whatever place you choose, make sure it won't add stress in the long run. The more stressed you become, the more difficult it would be to give it your best. As a means of improvising, you can create a plant hanger from a door handle, sellotape your dowel to the edge of a table and so many other ways.

Starting off with the right materials

You will find cotton a more convenient and easy to use material for creating macramé. I'm not saying that others are not suitable for you. I'm advising that as a learner, you start with materials that are soft and easy to handle. You can use them in quite a variety of color combinations and styles. It is recommended over nylon for its homely and comfortable traits. Another good option to start from would be the regular use of chunky wool. You should realize that it is safer to start your cord size with a three-millimeter diameter so that the key strings would fit for both plant hangers and small to medium wall hangings.

Overcome your fear of failures while knotting. If it doesn't look attractive enough to you, readjust it till it does. The more consistency you put in, the.more results you'll be able to achieve in quite a short period.

Another useful tip is that you should be aware of is that you should try to keep extra scraps as short as ten centimeters because you will eventually need them as you progress. Lengths shorter them that could be used as cushion fillings.

Try out easier projects

Everyone loves to head straight on to something serious and tedious when they haven't been made familiar with simple tasks. Making things as simple as key chains and hangers might seem insignificant, but they are a great and gently start for a beginner. As you accomplish more while trying to create beautiful designs of these, you can easily attempt more tasking projects. Even if it takes you quite a while trying to finish them, it becomes easier when you attempt it the second time. Other projects like macramé feathers require lesser skill and knotting. The feathers, however, might require much patience trying to brush and trim the sides into perfection.

Stay curious

For the success of any craft, the artist has to maintain a high level of curiosity. Curiosity is more or less an asset of gold while developing neat macramé designs. Your curiosity comes from your ability to keep getting inspired by the works of others. You can wrap yourself around other artists and works even if they seem abstract to you. You will need all the motivation you can get by viewing and learning from their artwork. As you try to replicate the same designs, you will become the very best.

Staying curious and open to new ideas is paramount to creativity. Expanding your resources—whether it's through free platforms like Pinterest or Instagram—will ensure that you have a diverse range of sources to pull from when needed.

A Short message from the Author:

Hey, I hope you are enjoying the book? I would love to hear your thoughts!

Many readers do not know how hard reviews are to come by and how much they help an author.

I would be incredibly grateful if you could take just 60 seconds to write a short review on Amazon, even if it is a few sentences!

>> Type this address https://amzn.to/3kdAcxX into your web browser to leave a quick review

Thanks for the time taken to share your thoughts!

Chapter 4

Getting Started with Macramé

Essential Materials and Tools Needed

Cord/Rope

As you begin your journey into the world of macramé, you need to understand the materials used in making your designs. One of such terms you need to get used to are cords and ropes. So many people don't know the various types of cords that are available. Good knowledge of this will help you choose a cord that suits your design the most. Many people assume that there are just plain ropes; they fail to realize that various fibers can be used in macramé designs. With that said, let's try to differentiate macramé ropes from cords, although they are sometimes used as synonyms.

Macramé ropes

These ropes are three-stranded ropes (also called three-ply) in which the strands are twisted around each other.

There could be as much as four strands, but the most common is the three-strand ropes. A macramé rope is stronger than a string. It gives better flexibility when untwisted. You would notice a full, wavy fringe as it unfolds, making a great choice when you seek to design with great texture.

Its strength makes it a good option for making furniture pieces so that weight can be supported easily. As time progresses, they tend to expand as much as 1mm in some climatic conditions.

Macramé cords

A macramé cord is a group of fiber and strands which are twisted and braided together. They can be used to create knots or just tied together to form macramé. It is sometimes referred to as yarns, ropes or strings. These names are just used to mean the same thing.

Macramé cords are mostly found in a six-strand braid. This has been around for a long time, even as the cotton string was disliked by many. Cotton macramé cords, also called sash was the major type of cord used at that time. Although stiff when in use, its strength has proven to be of immense benefit. Many weight-bearing pieces were crafted with the sash cotton cord.

Choosing Macramé Cord

There are three types of macramé cords, these include:

- Braided cords
- 3-ply / 3 Strands
- Single Strands

Any macramé cord you come across must fall into these categories mentioned.

Macramé Braided Cord

These are the type of macramé cords you will find in many stores and event centers, such as big-box retail stores, Wal-mart, Hobby lobby, et.c. People tend to purchase it faster than other forms of cords because it is cheaper and easy to work with. The rush you feel when you're working on a macramé project can drive you into specializing on braided cords without testing to see its suitability with the design or purpose for creating it. So, they start to discover that it would have been better if they made use of another type of cord. The braided cord is made up of a combination of cotton, nylon, polyester, polypropylene and other fibers. Its major strength lies in its ability to hold objects and tie things together. It might have serious difficulties when trying to re-knot and fringe.

The braided cord is a good choice when starting your journey in macramé. It helps you achieve more neat designs and satisfy the customer. As you grow, you will notice a transition from the braided cords to the 3-ply or the single straight cord. While the word "rope" might be used to mean a braided or 3-ply cord, the word cord encompasses both fibers, strings and ropes. The standard measuring diameter for macramé braided cords is 5mm, 6mm, 7mm and 8mm.

Macramé 3-Ply

A 3-ply cord can also be called a 3- strand cord. It is made up of three small strands that form into a large twisted rope. When you hear some mention three or four-ply cords, they are only trying to emphasize the number of strands that have been twisted to form one single strand of cord. The Bochiknot macramé cotton cord has the following standard diameter measurement: 3ply, 4ply, 3mm, 4mm, 5mm, 6mm, and 7mm.

A multiple is used to refer to macramé cords, which have more than three strands. Here you can have as much as six strands woven together to a single strand.

Macramé Single Strand Cord

Single strand cords are probably the best material type to use if you really want to venture into macramé as a hobby or full-time work. Due to their reliability and feel, they are more expensive than other categories of cords. If this would be too much of an expense on you, there are other inexpensive options like cotton cords. Whatever material you are using should be very flexible and comfortable to use. The single cords make cutting cords, tying and unraveling of knots much more easier and faster. The macramé single strand cotton cords have diameter measurements ranging from three millimeters to seven millimeters.

Since you understand the different types of macramé cords, you need to also know what key elements to look out for when choosing what kind of macramé cord will best fit the project you want to embark on.

Macramé Cord Composition

The classification of macramé cords, according to their composition, is divided into natural and synthetic fibers.

Natural fibers are fibers produced from naturally occurring sources. These sources could be in the form of plants, animals, or even some geological processes. Some plant and animal sources include cotton, linen, jute, wool and hemp.

The other classification is synthetic fibers. These are made from processed polymers and molecules. The compounds which the raw materials are gotten from are mainly petrochemicals. Examples of such would be nylon, polyesters and spandex.

Macramé Cord Texture

This includes the feel, touch, appearance, finish and texture of the cord. All these qualities make each cord type different from each other. Your ability to identify these traits in the different cords you use will make it easier to know which one to use for a particular project.

Macramé Cord Size

Small Macramé Cord

These range from 1-2mm in diameter. You can find them used in strings for holding jewelry, threads on beads and buttons. They should be used for crafting projects that need little or no details.

Medium Macramé Cord

These kinds of cords are so popular for creating a lot of macramé designs. They are available in 3 and 4mm, and they are great for making plant hangers, wall hangings, lanterns, curtains, rugs, and lots more.

Large Macramé Cord

They are used for large macramé projects. Their range begins from 6mm and above. Due to their size, they cover lots of space. Though the knots might be few, they must be large in size.

Beads

Bead types can be described and named from different angles. They could be categorized based on criteria such as:

- material
- shape
- production process
- origin
- surface pattern and;
- fashion trends

Types of Beads

Gemstone Beads

These can also be called semi-precious beads. They are gotten from natural gemstones, artificially created gemstones, or even reconstructed materials. They are available in various sizes and shapes all to suit whatever you have in mind. They are round in shape with sizes ranging from 4-12 mm. You can also get other shapes apart from the smooth round ones that are more common. They can be in the form of chips or irregular (e.g., amethyst, jade, agate)

Natural Pearls and Shells

These pearls either come from freshwater or saltwater. They exist in colors like pink, peach, mauve, white and sometimes creamy colors. You can also make use of glass pearls, which have the same features as consistency in size, color, shape and finishing.

Glass Beads

These types of beads have existed for a long time, dating as far as 3500 years ago. They were first discovered in Egypt because of their clear and colorful outlook. Today, we have many more varieties of this type of beads. A lot of them come from countries like Japan, Italy, Swarvoski and a lot more. China has also been able to come up with imitations that resemble glass beads (glass pearls).

Wooden Beads

These are by far the most common type of beads used in macramé projects. Different types of wood beads are being used and this classification is based on extra purposes they are used for. The following are the types of wooden beads and where they are gotten from.

- Greywood
- Jackfruit (Asia)
- Oak (Europe)
- Rosewood (Philippines)
- Patikan (Philippines)
- Bayong (Philippines) and;
- Palmwood

Crystal Beads (Swarovski)

These beads are made from lead glass and have a shining quality or effect. Their faces are faceted so that the shine it emits is more prominent. Among the most common are the Swarovski and Czech crystal, which have high quality and are sold at cheaper prices.

Bugle Beads

These beads have a tubular shape and cut to various lengths. They can also be classified among the seed group since they are small and can be used to create amazing patterns on the macramé design. They are available in different colors, finishes and twists. Their sizes are represented in small decimal diameters like 0.5,1,1.5,2,3 and 5. The bugle beads with sizes 2 and 3 are also equivalent in size with seed beads of size 11.

Crystals

An example of crystals used for macramé is the chaton and tivoli crystals. The chaton crystals are faceted and pinter back also foiled to make them sparkle. The tivoli crystals are quite circular with smooth facets that are pointed at the middle, front or back of the crystal. They are glued to the surface of the macramé project or bedazzled using seed beads.

Delica Beads (Miyuki)

These are small cylindrical and perfect shaped glass beads with thin walls with large holes. They are produced by the Miyuki's. They are produced in two sizes, 11 and 8 (which is often called the double delicate).

Faceted Beads

These beads are cut into many pieces to produce multiple flat faces so that a sparkling effect can be created. They are made from glass, examples being fire-polished beads and Rondelles. Rondelles are more compressed than round beads so that they fit well as spacers. You can use them for various finishing and sizes of designs. Some of them have crystals attached to them.

Seed Beads

Seed beads are made from chopped glass, which forms short pieces. The glass cane is heated so that it can create a smooth and round shape. This type of beads is found mostly in China, Czech or Japanese countries. Among all the leading countries where the production of this type of bead is predominant, Japan tops them all with the best quality of seed beads. Czech and China follow behind with moderate and cheap irregular seed beads. Also found among the family of the seed beads are the delicate beads, square beads, hex and bugle beads.

Rocaille/ Round Beads

These round beads are sold from sizes 3 to size 15. They are used for stitching beadwork and can be used as spacers for macramé projects. If you want to get quality Rovaille beads, you will patronize Toho and Miyuki manufacturing brands. Their beads are consistent in shape, size and color.

Shamballa Style Beads

These beads are made with a clay base, decorated with some Czech crystals which are set closely together on the surface to give a sparking and eye-catching design. They are commonly used to make styled bracelets in macramé implementation of the square knotting technique.

Lamp Worked Beads

These beads are also another type of beads that are hand made by melting glass rods with a flaming torch. The hot glass is then wrapped around a coated wire. As the glass is removed, this bead is formed. They can be made with various colors and layers.

Wood or Dowels

These are another great composition for your macramé projects. Many people just have them stacked around the house without realizing their significance. They are far more useful in a good number of projects apart from macramé.

1. Cord, twine, or rope dispenser (depending on thickness)

    You can have a dowel attached to a wooden piece, wood scrap and also handy dispensers and organizers for spool and twines with similar materials.

2. Hanging, drape, or tablecloth weight

   Dowels can also be used in the clothing industry to weight down the bottom of textiles. You need them when you want the bottom hems to fit properly without any need for modifications.

   They will ensure that the textile doesn't drift when the airflow increases.

3. Ribbon and wrapping organizer

   In order to create ribbons, wrapping papers and other items that unfurled without creating any mess, you need to make use of dowels. You attach them to backing boards wrapped with leftover wrapping paper so that a tight space can be created around the dowel. You can use movable tags to ensure that the paper remains in its place.

4. Grout spreader

   In residential buildings, you would have noticed that tiles installed in complex patterns in hard to reach areas need a form of material or equipment like a dowel. A dowel will help you distribute the tiles in the manner or pattern you choose wherever you need to fix them.

5. Roller

   Since dowels have a round shape, we can make use of them to our advantage by using them as rolling pins for domestic and catering uses. You achieve this by pressing down the diesel on the material you want to roll, either flat or round. You can use them as a roller for whatever form of cooking materials to create your desired shape, feel and taste.

6. Dowel joints

   You've probably heard that one of the common ways a dowel can be used is as a joining material. This is mainly done in woodwork projects where you need to ring several joints together and create a form of reinforcement. Dowels are used at this point as pegs inside the wood joint. As you attach them to your woodwork joints, they add strength and reduce the number of seams and hardware you need outside the joint. Carpenters use this more often to add flexibility and better finishing to their projects.

7. Workshop organizing

Dowels are a good tool for organizing pegs on walks to hang tools, equipment and supplies. This can keep your garages and workshops arranged and looking safer. When equipments are littered all over your workspace, they can constitute grave danger and accidents. It helps you access tools and spare parts faster since you already know where you've kept them.

8. Added shelf support

Other stout dowels are used as braces for shelves in bookshelves and support to an already stuffed shelf (especially one loaded with heavy books). Your dowels can be cut to different shapes and sizes depending on the type of shelf it needs to be attached to. This is to ensure that the shelves don't sag as pressure increases.

9. Cheap curtain hangers

   As curtain hangers, dowels are great substitutes for curtain rods. You can even make them more attractive by adding fancy finials to them. All these are at a cheap and affordable rate. The choice of dowel is according to the type and length of fabric to be used. The dowel should be able to support the weight of the material, e.g., canvas, velvet. Dowels can also be used as sliders in window locks to ensure extra security.

10. Tool rehabilitation

    If you have a broom tool with a handle where you notice movement in the wrong direction, you can use a dowel to bring it back to proper working condition by detaching the already worn out part and replacing it with a dowel of appropriate thickness. This is far more cheaper when you compare it with replacing the tool handle.

How to choose a dowel

Before we can pick a dowel suitable for making macramé designs, we need to first understand where the dowels come from. Dowels are wooden structures that may aid as support to your macramé project. They are gotten from tree parts. Examples include the birch, cherry, oak trees. Most times dowels are cut from hardwoods such as beech, mahogany and beach trees. On other occasions, we fall back to the softwoods, e.g., pine.

Differences between hardwood and softwood

Hardwoods are woods cut from trees that have leaves. These trees can also be called deciduous trees because they loose their leaves during the winter season. Softwoods, on the other hand, are timber gotten from trees that have needles in them or what you would probably call evergreen trees. They are evergreen because irrespective of the season, their leaves still remain.

The idea that softwoods are soft is more of a speculation than a statement of fact. Some hardwoods are actually softer than most softwoods. An example of this would be the pine, which is stronger than most softwoods. Differentiation is more of the source than the texture of the wood.

Woods that have more density have a higher resistance to breaking and are a good supplement for joints and can hold macramé weights. Woods that have higher density include the oak, cherry and beech trees. Density measurements are indicated in both empirical and metric units.

Another factor to consider while choosing dowels is the color. This only becomes an issue when the dowel is to be visible when the project is completed. Color choice is more of personal preference. Some people might prefer lighter colors while others deep and dark colors.

Adhesive Tapes

Adhesive tapes are a combination of materials and films which help hold and join objects together instead of using fasteners. Some macramé projects would require the use of adhesive tapes to hold in place some decorative materials, e.g., beads. This helps avoid the use of high-temperature measures to ensure that different components are put together. Adhesive tapes also protect the surface area of materials since there is no need to use extra fasteners to hod the materials in place. It is more preferable to use them instead of liquid adhesives, which are more time consuming since they need to be sprayed or rolled on the surface before any bonding can occur.

Adhesive tapes are made up of a material called backing or carrier, e.g., cloth, paper, plastic film, foam e.t.c. It may be coated with a liner if the need arises. The coated backing/carrier is wound to form rolls of tapes. The roll can be placed into narrow width bands so that the rolls are duplicated. Every roll is different from each other and can be used for specific allocations while designing macramé projects.

Types of adhesive tapes

Pressure-sensitive tapes

These types of adhesive tapes are very sticky at normal temperatures when in dry form. You can use them on a number of surfaces and only require little pressure with the finger or hand. They don't require water, solvents and heats to establish bonds. They have a specified pressure and the temperature range beyond or below which binding will be difficult. The temperature range for application is between 59-95 °F. When the temperature is below this, there will be insufficient coverage over the material. High temperatures will lead to stretching of the tape which will lead to an ineffective bond.

Heat tapes

These categories of adhesive tapes can also be used for macramé projects. The problem with this type of tapes is that they must be used with the application of heat. The heat you know is very detrimental to the safety of the project since the knotting materials are made from wools, cotton and other light materials. It is, therefore, not advisable to use such for any bonding materials to your macramé designs. The temperatures required for bonding lie above 180°F.

Water adhesive tapes

For these, they perform better when the material to be bonded is lighter and has little size. They are starch-based adhesives that become sticky by the application of water. This forms a mixture which is applied on the surface of the macramé before adding another material

Other nonadhesive tapes do not require an adhesive because they can bond by themselves with any material they come in contact with. A good example of such would be the PTFE thread sealing tape.

Materials used as carriers of adhesive tapes

Every adhesive tape has a carrier or backing material. Here are some of the types of carriers you will find;

Paper: These are also referred to as flatback tapes.

Cloth: This may be in the form of woven cloth or fabric, which acts as a reinforcement for extra strength and resistance to heat.

Felt: These are found in adhesive tapes without a backing. They are specially designed to prevent scratching of surfaces.

Foam: This type of coating on adhesive tapes is made so that the tape can be protected from some weather and chemical processes while sealing or mounting.

Metal foil: These carriers are installed as a preventive measure against fires and high-temperature effects. This type of adhesive tape isn't used for macramé projects, but since we are giving you an overview of what carries you might find in adhesive tapes, it is important that you take note of them.

Other categories of adhesive tapes include:

Plastic films: There are two types of plastics, thermoplastics and thermosets. This type of adhesive tapes contains more than one layer composed of a plastic film. The layers are usually clear, printed or

This also can be used for assembly works like gripping, twisting and bending. They are the most common pliers.

Slip Joint Pliers

They are used for adjusting nuts and bolts.

End Cutting Pliers

As the name goes, you can use them to cut wires, nails, rivets.

Things to note while using pliers in macramé projects

Ensure that before you make use of them, you cover your eyes and face with some material, either glass or shield, especially when using it on hard surfaces like wood and metals. This will prevent particles from entering your eyes and other parts of your face.

Ensure that whatever you cut is at a right angle with the plier. Bending back and forth could be dangerous.

Your plier should be adjustable enough to firmly grip the workpiece even as you maintain a good handgrip.

If you notice rusts or difficulty while using it, please take it for greasing or change it if need be. The cutting edges need to be sharp, not dull, so that you don't exert so much pressure and energy getting a material cut. Ensure that you check if they are in good condition before you attempt using them so that you can avoid the injuries that will result from a stiff or rusty plier.

Knotting Boards

Knotting boards are another great tool you need while trying to craft macramé. They are important because sometimes, you may have trouble holding knots and helms together. This can only be done with attachments made on the knotting board. However, some persons feel that macramé should be done in the old fashioned way and not with any type of implementations. Nonetheless, you will need them, especially if you need to be very detailed with thread works. Its use, however, depends on what type of macramé project you are constructing. For more serious projects like wall hangers, suspended tables and plant hangers, you will most likely need them.

Knotting board is a simple board with the texture of foam board or heavy corrugated cardboard, which is strong enough to hold your project together with T pins. This way, you'll be able to make your knots tight, neat and nice. Since most of the knots you will be making use of are square and double half hitches knots, a knotting board can help you hold your cords even as you create them. This is possible because of the slashes that are embedded in them. This makes knotting a lot more easier to handle.

Metal Ring or Hoops

Metal rings can be used in your macramé projects to create mandalas, wreaths, earrings and other wall hangings such as plant hangers. If you intend to make plant hanger loops and other hanging macramé designs, small metal rings would be a great fit. However, if you will be hanging anything heavy, ensure that the chosen ring is welded closed so that it is strong enough to hold the weight of your macramé design.

Measuring Tape

This is used for measuring the length of the macramé cord.

Tape

These are used to tape the ends of the macramé cords. As for me, I use painters tape because they are super easy to remove, but masking tape would also suffice. However, if you would rather not use tape, the ends of the cords can be sealed by melting with a candle flame.

Chapter 5

Macramé Projects for Home Decoration

Macramé Hanging Chair

Hanging chairs are a new improvement to the luxury and comfort of many homes today. Aside from their applications in homes, they can also be used for the backyard patio or garden. There are many places where you can hang your macramé chairs, such as on the ceiling or on a stand. They are also an alternative to the hammock because they require less space and can be hung up virtually anywhere. Due to the creativity involved in crafting them, they find their application in various decoration purposes.

The macramé knots used to make this design are square knot, lark's head knot, double half hitch, and spiral knots, making the level of difficulty relatively low. However, this DIY project can become really complicated, depending on the design you select for the seat and backrest.

What you will need

- Braided Macramé cord, approx. 200m
- 2 rods or dowel with c-ends
- Two metal hoops, one 70 cm, and the other 110 cm

Instructions

The Seat

Begin with the seat, using the 70 cm metal hoop/ ring.

The Backrest

Place the rods in-between the seat and the backrest, as given below, then knot the two hoops together, as shown in the diagram.

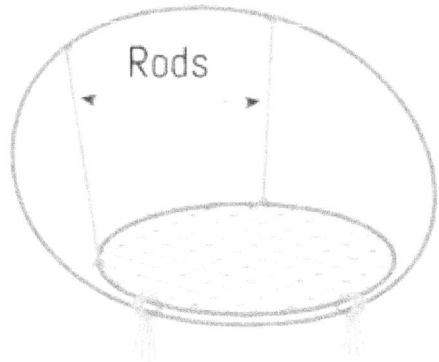

Following the pattern below, knot the ends to the seat.

Backrest

Assemble the Macramé Hanging Chair

Once you are finished, wrap each hoop with a cord. When you do, the ends of the knotted cords will be secured. Likewise, pass the cord knotting the two rings to join them. Cut cords and have them mounted on the back of the seat. Following the decoration pattern, tie them.

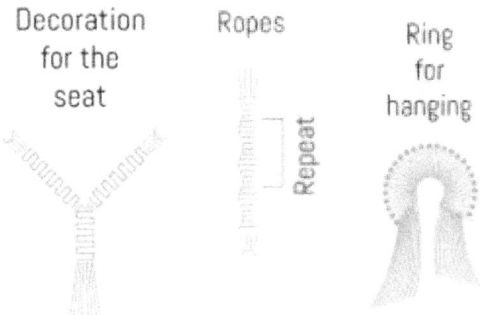

Hang the Chair

To hang the chair, four ropes would have to be made using the spiral knot technique. 8 cords will be required, 4 of which would be twice the length needed plus 50 cm and the other 4 cords will be three times the desired length.

To begin, make a loop fold and fixing the threads to the chair. The short strips should be tied to the backrest, while the longer ones should be in the front. Begin your spiral knots and continue until you reach the desired length. Then, gather all the threads, tying them into a loop and allow the ends to hang at different lengths.

Brass Ring Macramé Dream Catcher

Based on so many myths, it is believed that dream catchers have the potency to prevent bad dreams and nightmares. Today, they have become an acceptable decoration. You can even gift them to your loved ones to show how much you care and love them. We'll be looking at how you can make dream catchers with the following steps below to guide you through.

What you will need

- Cotton macramé cord

- 10" brass ring
- Scissors
- Measuring tape or yard stick

Instructions

Attaching the Cord to the Ring

To start, cut 10 pieces of macramé cord of length 8 feet. Tie each piece of the cord to a brass ring using lark's knot. To do this, you fold the cord into two and place the folded bit under the loop. Bring the ends of the cord over the hoop and through the folded part before tightening (refer to the section on Macramé Knots and Patterns).

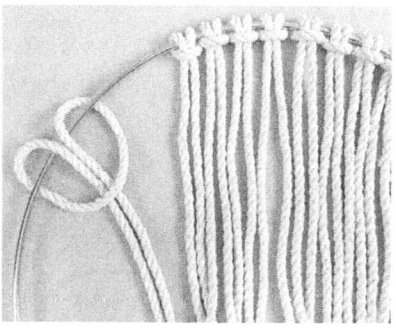

This is the finished work after you must have attached all ten cords to the hoop with a lark's head knot.

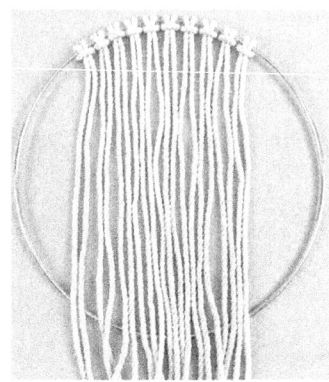

Square Knot

The next step involves a square knot to make the triangle section of the pattern. Tie the square knots on 4 cords (two in the center and two outer cords used for the tying). The center knots will be stationary while the other outer knots are tied to it.

You begin working with the four cords on the far left while moving all other cords off to the side so that you avoid confusion.

Your first step would be to make a number four shape with the cord in the far left, bring it under the two center cords and over the right cord.

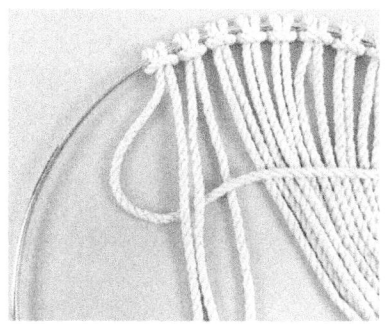

Next, bring the right cord over the two center cords and through the number shape. You can pull the cords to tighten.

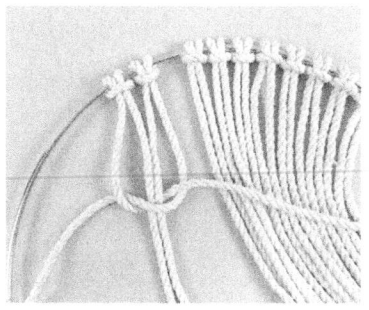

Next, you make a letter P shape with the right cord, bring it under the two center cords and over to the left cord.

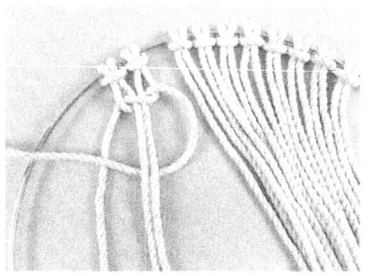

Finally, take the left cord over the two center cords and through the loop made by the letter P.

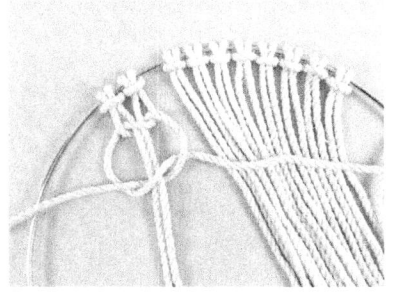

After this, pull and tighten; the center cords will experience a tug. This is because the cords aren't knotted to anything. The cords can also be bunched up. Bunching gives a better appeal to your project and you also need to tug after the knot is completed.

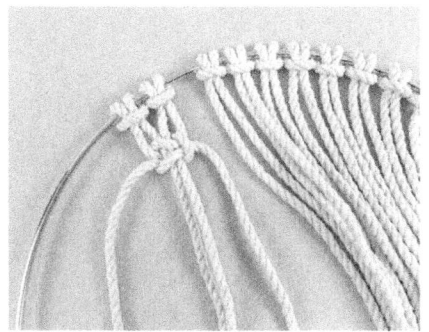

When this is completed, the square knot is continued on all the four cords across the entire group.

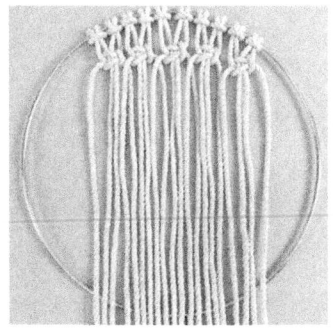

To make a triangle shape on the design, you decrease the number of knots in each row. With this done, you will leave two strands on the far left off to the side unworked. Your knotting should begin with the strands that are available, which number up to four. With these strands, you can tie the square knot just as you did previously. This square knot will make use of the two strands from each of the knots done previously. As you continue the process, a lattice pattern will emerge. Continue across the rows by leaving the two strands on the far right unworked

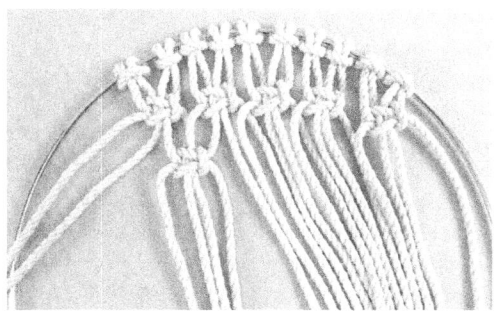

Leave two extra strands unworked at the end of each row until you reach the last row. You will discover that you have left just one knot in the center. At this stage, this is how the finished work should look.

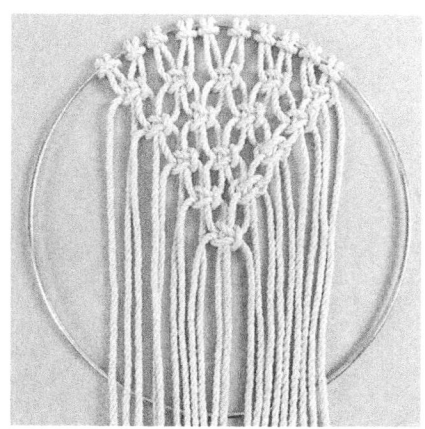

The next stage is to knot the diagonal double half hitch borders.

Diagonal Double Half-Hitch Border

First, begin by making an end along the triangle using the diagonal double half hitch knot. To start, pick the first cord on both sides, whether left or right (the part you start with doesn't really matter), then lay down the cord diagonally across all the other cords.

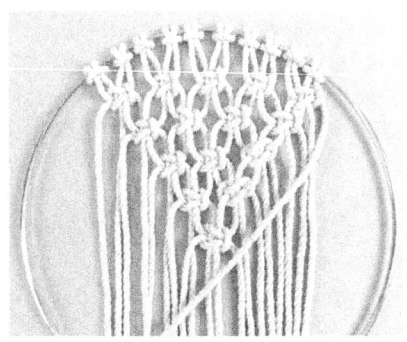

Next, take the available cord and bring it under the diagonal cord and through the loop and pull till it becomes tight. You will repeat this knot in the opposite direction using the two cords you began with.

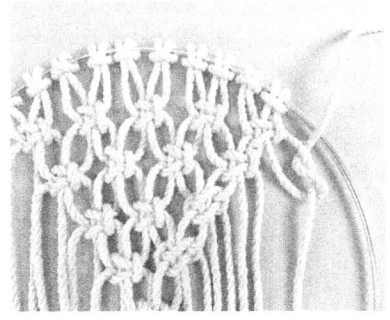

As you continue this repetition, you will begin to notice the formation of the triangle.

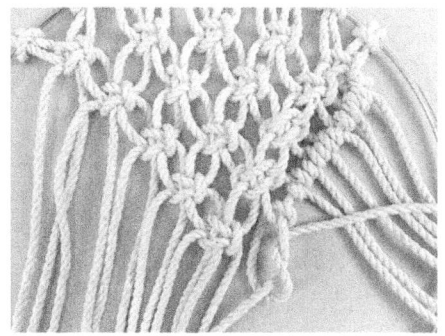

Repeat the pattern on the other side of the triangle so that you will just be left with two strands dangling in the center. You should tie these cords together in a half hitch knot so that the triangle can be completed.

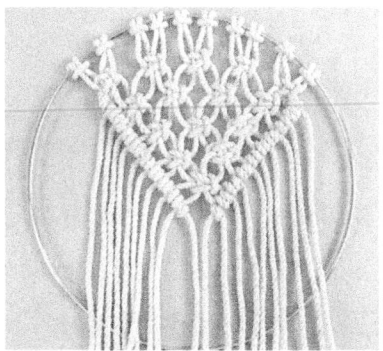

Attaching to the Bottom of the Ring

Since every other part of the project has been completed, we move on to the bottom sides of the ring.

Move all the cords you have to the back of the ring and tie each cord to form a double half hitch knot as you have done earlier. The knots should be done directly on the ring. With this, your dream catcher is completed.

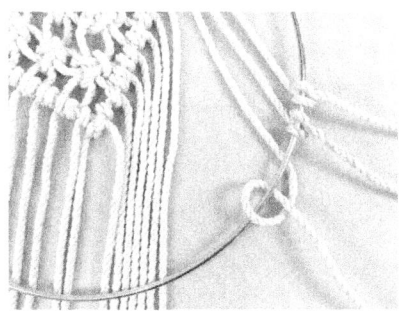

Macramé Wall Hanging

Macramé, quite alright, can be a daunting craft at first. Hence, I have created this DIY macramé wall hanging for beginners. This macramé project uses just four types of macramé knots, most of which have already been discussed on.

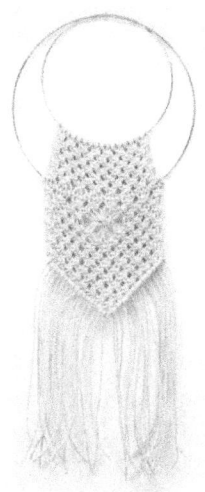

Below, I provide you with step-by-step instructions on how to make this beautiful macramé project in no time.

Knots you will need

- Lark's head knot
- Square knot
- Double square knot (This is the same as the square knot; it just has twice as many cords used in the square knot – refer to the section on knots and patterns).
- Double half hitch knot (This is the same as the hitch knot; it just has twice as many cords used in

hitch knot – refer to the section on knots and patterns)

What you will need

- 160 ft. of macramé cord (3mm thick)
- Scissors
- 10" gold hoop
- 14" gold hoop
- Tape measure

Instructions

Step 1: Cut the macramé cord into sixteen 10-foot pieces

Using the tape measure, a 10 ft of macramé cord should be measured out. Once a 10ft piece is measured and cut, use it to measure out the rest.

Step 2: Tie onto the 10-inch hoop, 16 lark's head knots.

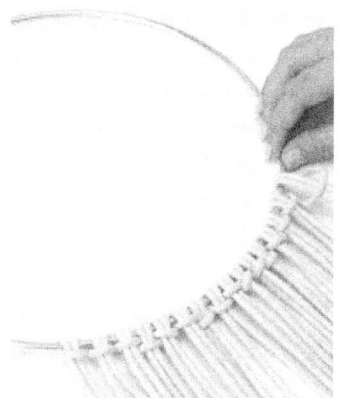

Step 3: Create square knots of 7 rows, while you alternate between tying 7 and 8 knots.

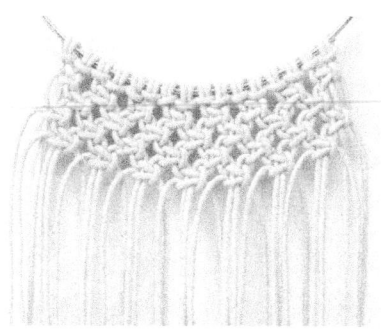

In this tutorial, the leftmost cord is the 1st cord

Row 1: Begin with the 1st cord — and tie 8 square knots

Row 2: Begin with the 3rd cord — and tie 7 square knots

Row 3: Begin with the 1st cord — and tie 8 square knots

Row 4: Begin with the 3rd cord — and tie 7 square knots

Row 5: Begin with the 1st cord — and tie 8 square knots

Row 6: Begin with the 3rd cord — and tie 7 square knots

Row 7: Begin with the 1st cord — and tie 8 square knots

Step 4: Each of the 32 cords should be attached beneath the 14-inch hoop with a double half hitch knot.

Row 8: Begin with the 1st cord — and tie 32 **double half hitch knots** to the hoop.

Step 5: Continue to tie square knots and double square knots for 16 extra rows.

Row 9: Begin with the 1st cord — and tie 8 square knots

Row 10: Begin with the 3rd cord — and tie 3 square knots, skipping 4 cords, then tie 3 square knots

Row 11: Begin with the 1st cord — and tie 3 square knots, skipping 8 cords, then tie 3 square knots

Row 12 Begin with the 3rd cord — and tie 2 square knots, skipping 2 cords. Tie 1 double square knot, skipping 2 cords, then tie 2 square knots

Row 13: Begin with the 1st cord — and tie 3 square knots, skipping 8 cords, then tie 3 square knots

Row 14: Begin with the 3rd cord — and tie 3 square knots, skipping 4 cords, then tie 3 square knots

Row 15: Begin with the 1st cord — and tie 8 square knots

Row 16: Begin with the 3rd cord — and tie 7 square knots

Row 17: Begin with the 1st cord — and tie 8 square knots

Row 18: Begin with the 3rd cord — and tie 7 square knots

Row 19: Begin with the 5th cord — and tie 6 square knots

Row 20: Begin with the 7th cord — and tie 5 square knots

Row 21: Begin with the 9th cord — and tie 4 square knots

Row 22: Begin with the 11th cord — and tie 3 square knots

Row 23: Begin with the 13th cord — and tie 2 square knots

Row 24: Begin with the 15th cord — and tie 1 square knot

Step 6: Tie 16 diagonal half hitch knots beginning with the cord on the rightmost side

A diagonal half hitch knot is also the same as a regular half hitch knot. However, instead of it being tied around the hoop, you will tie it around another string. Take the cord on the rightmost side (32nd), crossing it

over the other cords to the left. Begin with cord 31st, tying 15 half hitch knots to cord 32nd.

Row 25: Begin with cord 31st — and tie to the left, 15 diagonal half hitch knots.

Step 7: Starting with the leftmost cord, tie 16 diagonal half hitch knots

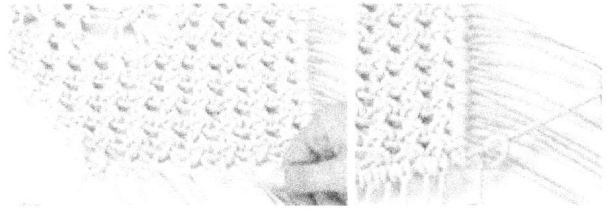

Repeat step 6 above on the opposite side, and cross the cord on the leftmost side over the cords to the right. Tie half hitch knots to the cord.

Row 25: Begin with the 1st cord — and tie to the right, 16 diagonal half hitch knots.

Step 8: Trim the end of the cords, then hang in your favorite spot of your house.

Macramé Room Divider

Partitions have been in long use for dividing rooms into separate spaces. With this, you can have a door granting access to the various sections of the room. Macramé dividers are a better and more artistic way of achieving the same results.

Apart from the fashionable side if it, macramé dividers economize the space and make sure that the divisions are not more than expected measurement.

What you will need

- 1" x 36" wooden dowel
- 700 ft of 1/4" 3 strand cotton rope
- Three 3 inch hook screws
- Scissors
- Air plants (optional)

Instructions

Preparing Your Rope

You start by measuring 24 strands, 28 inches long each. This ensures wall hanging measures seven inches from the top dowel to the bottom of the dowel. You can decide to add more lengths with a fringe at the bottom. It is better to add more lengths when measuring your rope.

Lark's Head Knot

Using the lark's head knot tutorial in the knots and pattern section, make a replica of the lark's head knot shown above, taking note of the 12 knots total that is needed.

Half Knot

The next step is to add half knots. It requires 4 strands of rope. After successfully knotting the half knots, the first section of the divider has been completed, as shown below

Square Knot

The square knot is the next stage. It comprises two half knots, so what you do is to repeat the same steps you used earlier, but this time pull the outer ropes until to second-half knot rests against the first half knot. As you repeat this process, you will form the rows of knots.

If you did this according to instructions, you should be having twelve square knots in the first row.

Alternating Square Knot

To create a second row of square knots, use two strands from the first square knot and two from the second square knot next to it to create a new square knot, joining them together.

Start in the middle of your piece, working your way out on either side or begin from one side, moving your way to the next. When you get to the edges of your second row, there will be an extra pair of rope strands on both sides.

Knots on the Edge

For my pattern, I did four alternating rows of square knots and then switched it up and did six alternating rows of half knots. Then I finished up the rest of the divider with 13 alternating rows of square knots again. This kept things feeling consistent enough to make a statement but also added a bit of a subtle design change to keep it from looking like I'd hung a hammock from the ceiling!

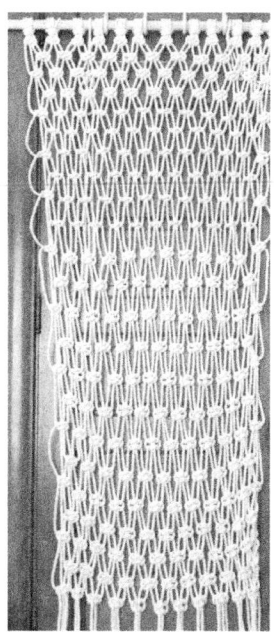

Adding the bottom dowel to your room divider requires that you create extra lark's head knots. This can be created just the way you started, but backward. See below for instructions.

A: Spead out four strands beneath one of your square knots, then set two aside.

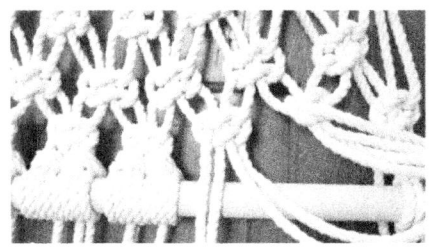

B: Use the other two strands to wrap around the dowel until the inside and over the top of the same two strands have been wrapped.

C: Wrap them on the other side of the strands and back behind the dowel.

D: Continue around the front of the dowel, tucking beneath the loop you just made. This will leave a fringe below the dowel's backside.

E: Bring each of the other two strands from the square knot back over, wrapping them around the dowel and to the left side.

F: Wrap them over the top of themselves.

G: Wrap them behind the dowel and all around and under the loop just created.

H: Scoot the knot in beside the first one you initially made. Repeat using the other strands in each square knot.

When done, trim your fringe to your desired length.

Macramé Mirror Wall Hanger

Macramé mirror hangers are hangers that are made from knotting techniques to hold the mirror in place.

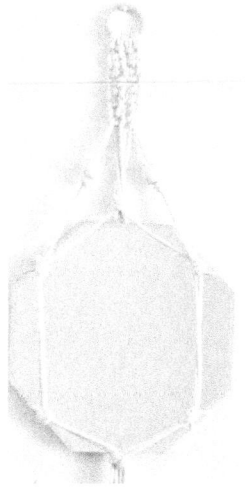

What you will need

- Macramé cord of length 4mm
- Octagon mirror
- Wood ring of length 2 inch
- Wood beads of 25mm w/10mm hole size
- Scissors

Instructions:

Step 1: Cut 108 inches of Macramé cords into 4 pieces each.

Step 2: Fold the strips in half. Using a lark's head knot, tie all 4 on the wood ring, then pull the knots tight and beside each other. Spread out two of the lark's head knots, then begin to tie them into a square knot.

Step 3: Begin to tie two square knots into the second two lark's head knots.

Step 4: As you begin the second square knot, loop it across one side of the other two square knots to form a larger square knot. Tie 7 square knots descending on both sides and altogether.

Step 5: The ends should be split off upon tying the knots—two strings for both sides and 4 in the middle. Tape should be added to the ends of the cord to seal the frayed ends, thus making it easy to add the beads.

Step 6: One bead should be added to both sides of the 2 side cording lines, while a knot should be made

beneath the bead on both sides to make them even by tying the center 4 cords into a plain knot about 1/14 inch beneath the beads.

Step 7: One cord from the center should be taken and added to the 2 cords on both sides. Then tie the three cords altogether in a knot on the two sides. Now, the mirror should be added so that the knot lengths become even. One of the 3 side cordings should be added to the back of the mirror for a firm grip. Tie a simple knot in all the 3 sides of the cords beneath the left and right side of the mirror. Separate the 3 sides cords again, take one on both side and place behind the mirror. Bring 2 on both sides to the front of the mirror, tying them into a knot.

Step 8: Turn over the mirror, tying all cords together. Turn the mirror back over to loosen the front knot. At this point, the back cords should be slipped inside the knot and retightened. Cut the ends of the cord to 14 inches. Pull the ends or let the cords be loosened, and let them fray. Hang and enjoy!

Easy Macramé Plant Hanger

Macramé designs are also good for creating plant hangers for your home and interior spaces. There are various types of macramé plant hangers that can be used for decorative purposes. One of such is the cotton macramé plant hanger. It is a more common macramé plant hanger. This plant hanger is woven by combining both cotton and nylon. They are all knotted together to produce 4 legs, an open basket where the plants are held. They can measure up to eight inches in length, and eighteen inches tassel hung below the planter.

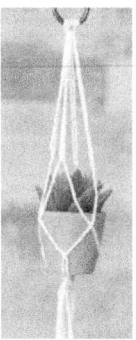

Another example of macramé plant hangers is the mkono colorful macramé plant hangers. This is a better choice for adding color to your macramé design. The mkono macramé plant hanger has a hook from which it can be hung on the ceiling. They help brighten the room and add a splash of colors.

The boho-chic macramé hanger is another plant hanger found in some homes. It measures fifty inches from where it is hung to the bottom of its component. Its tightly woven knot runs down from the rings to the braided basket large enough to house a 9-inch diameter pot. It is mostly used for indoor purposes due to its availability in natural colors. For the purpose of this section, we would focus on how to make a simple macramé plant hanger.

What you will need

- Metal or wooden ring
- Yarn
- Scissors
- Potted plant

Instructions

Step 1: Cut out 4 equal lengths of yarn. Mine was 2 ft, so ensure you have enough length to complete your Macramé plant holder.

Step 2: Your yarn strands should be folded in half, looping the folded end across the metal or wooden ring. Pull and taut the loose ends across the loop of the yarn you created.

Step 3: Spead out the yarn into a grouping of 4, 2 strands of yarn each.

Step 4: Measure out several inches, tying each of the groupings to each other. Ensure the knots are roughly the same length.

Step 5: Take the left strand from each of the groupings, tying it just to the right strand next to it. Tie the knots a bit higher, just an inch or two from the first knot set. Then take the two outermost strands, tying them to each other to form a circular net sort of.

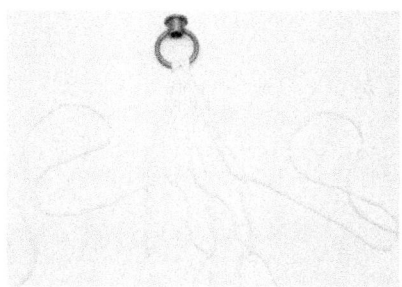

Step 6: Tie an additional set of knots by repeating the procedure in step 5 but make the knots quite close to the last set you did – with about half-inch or two away this time.

Step 7: All the yarn strands should be tied up in a knot just a bit beneath the last set of knots you made – an inch approximately. Excess yarn should be cut off to form a pretty tassel!

That's it! Simply slip in your planter into the Macramé plant holder.

Macramé Table Runners

Your table decoration isn't complete without table runners placed on it. Macramé table runners are an effective way of adding spice to your dining halls. They protect your table from spills and food damages that may occur when hot pans and candle wax are placed on it. Table runners find their application daily and can also be used for special occasions and events.

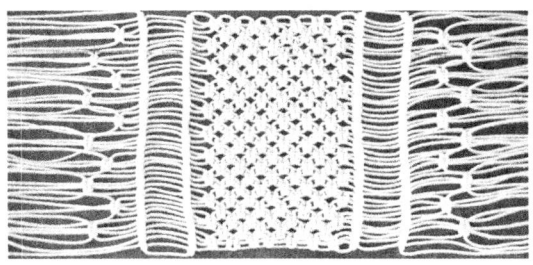

They give your table space a subtle and dramatic design even with the variation that is possible with the color and texture of materials. Your table runners could also be designed in such a way that other elements are added to mark the festive season. For example, your runners could be customized to fit the holiday season, such as Christmas or some sort of celebration.

What you will need

- 12" wooden dowel
- 22 strands of 16' cotton rope, measuring 3mm
- Door hooks
- 2" of cotton twine for dowel hanger
- Scissors

Instructions

Step 1: For the first step, tie cotton twines to your dowel and hang them from a door hook. Fold the strands of rope into two and create a lark's head knot.

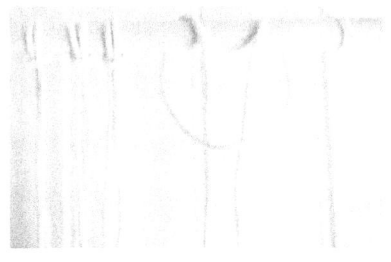

Step 2: The next step involves you adding 16' ropes using lark's head knot until you have a total of 22, giving a total of 44 strands.

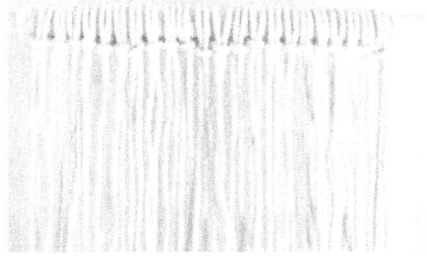

Step 3: Next, pull the outer right rope through the front of other ropes (to the left-hand side) and drape the end of your door hook. Use the second rope from the right-hand side to tie a single knot around the rope you just dapped. Ensure it is 6-inch below the dowel.

Step 4: Use the same strand to tie another knot over the base. This is what forms the half hitch knot. Make sure they are consistent.

Step 5: Repeat the same process for the other ropes from the outside. You will begin to see the pattern which emerges; it is a horizontal half hitch.

Step 6: Continue tying the ropes in consecutive manners to create a single knot across. You should allow the rope to be tied so tight that it pulls the edges.

Step 7: Begin again from the right and use the outer four strands to create a square knot below your horizontal

line of knots. Continue skipping four strands and tying the next four strands until you get across.

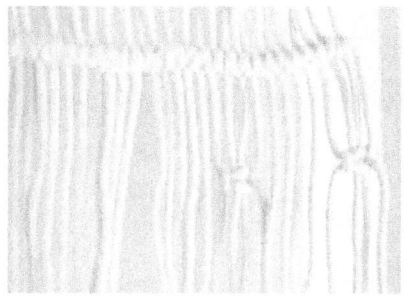

Step 8: On the right side, use the skipped knots to tie square knots 3-inch below the dowel. Continue to tie in square knots, the skipped four strands until the row is finished.

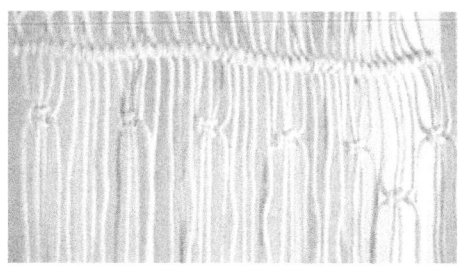

Step 9: Pull the outer strands on the right to the left, then use strands 3-6 strands to create another square knot below the horizontal row of knots. Use the next four strands to create an additional square knot 1.5-inch

higher than the last square knot and continue all the way across. Do nothing with the last two strands.

Step 10: Beginning from the right-hand side, an additional row of horizontal half-hitch knots should be created by repeating the steps 3-7 above.

Step 11: Use the same base strands to create an additional horizontal half hitch row knots beneath the

last one (about 2.5-inch). This time, the movement should be from left to right.

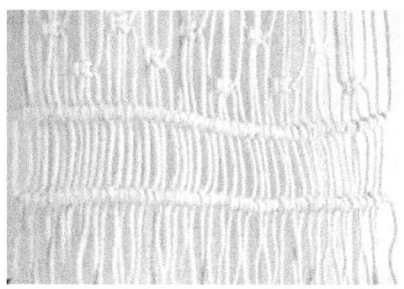

Step 12: Beginning from the left, create a row of square knots without skipping any strands resting below the horizontal line of knots. The second row of square knots should be done by skipping the first two left strands and tying another row of square knots. Keep on repeating these processes so that you have thirteen rows of alternating square knots.

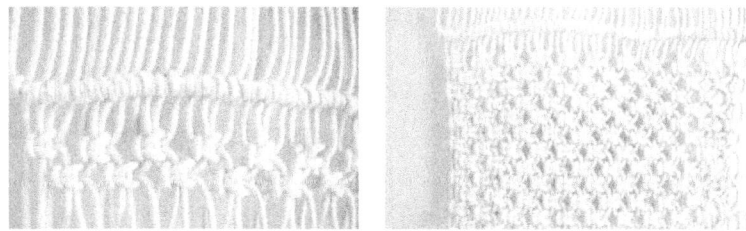

Step 13: Another half-hitch horizontal row of knots should be added, beginning from the outer left-hand side to the right-hand side.

Step 14: Move 2.5-inch downwards, using the same base rope to make an additional half-hitch horizontal row of knots from right to left.

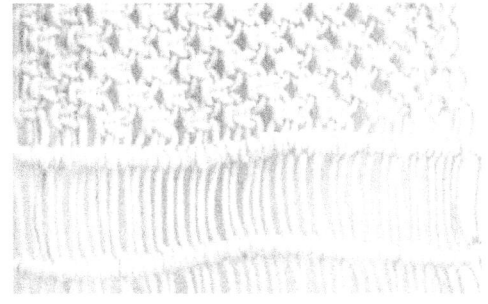

Step 15: Leave out the outer two strands of rope on the right-hand side, tying a square knot with strands three to strand six. Skip seven to ten strands and use eleven to fourteen strands to tie another square knot. Repeat such that every four strands are skipped. You should have six strands available on the left side.

Also, rows one and two should be skipped on the left side, then tie strands three to six using a square knot of 1.5-inch beneath that last row of square knots. Skip the next four strands, and then the pattern should be finished for the second row of square knots. This should avail you with six extra strands on the right side.

Step 16: Measure out 11-inch from the last row of horizontal knots and then tie a square knot with the outer four strands on the right-hand side. Tie the next four strands into a square knot with about 1.5-inch higher than the last knot. Repeat all the way across.

Step 17: Lastly, one last horizontal row of half-hitch knots should be tied about 1.5-inch beneath the row of alternating square knots. Trim the ends to your desired length. Take out the cotton twine away from the dowel and then slip off all the lark's head knots gently.

Cut the middle of the lark's head knot loop, trimming up the ends.

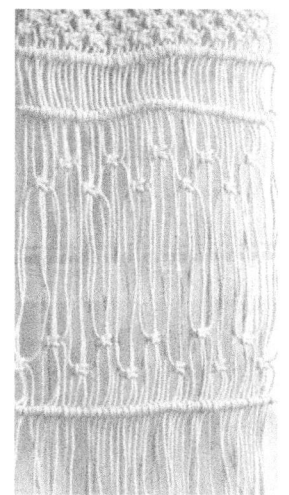

Chapter 6

Other Macramé Project Designs

Openwork Macramé Bracelets

If you are a lover of fashion, bracelets are something you cannot do without. They can be worn for different purposes and forms. They add color and class to your outfit and general look. No wonder they transform your appearance. You can wear them to match various shirt patterns and colors.

Macramé can also be used to make light and lacy looks, like this bracelet below.

This openwork macramé design is pretty, delicate, and faster to knot than a more dense pattern would be. To make a simple bracelet like the one shown above, follow the instructions below.

What you will need

- 10 crochet cotton
- Clasp
- Jump rings
- Large rings – about 1/2 inch or 12-14mm
- Scissors
- Sewing pins
- Cork panels
- Jewelry pliers
- Fray check or clear fabric glue

Choose the length of your intended bracelet (either in inches or in centimeters) before you start. Multiply the length by 11, then add an additional 12 inches or 30 cm. Cut out 8 strands of this length

Instructions:

Step 1: Pin down a large ring for firmness, then fold a strand into half. Make a lark's head knot and repeat three more times.

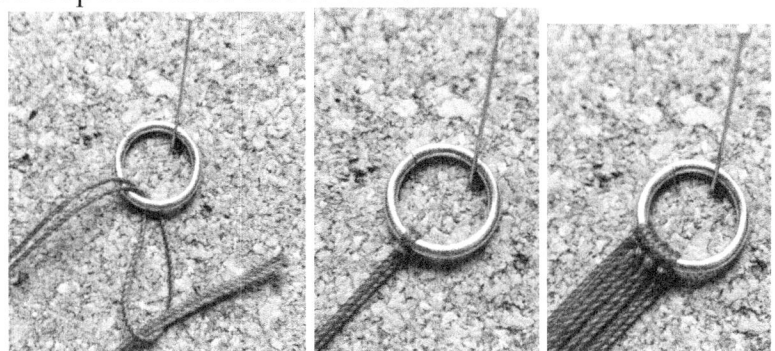

Step 2: Bring the strand at the far left, right through the rest, and tie a double half hitch knot all through it with the strand beside it. Also, tie a double half hitch with the rest of the strands.

Step 3: Bring the strand on the left side across, then tie an extra row of double half hitch knots.

Step 4: Repeat one more time. There should now be three rows, as shown below.

Step 5: Repeat the same on the right, but on the opposite side. Bring the strand on the far right across, then tie three rows of double half hitch knots.

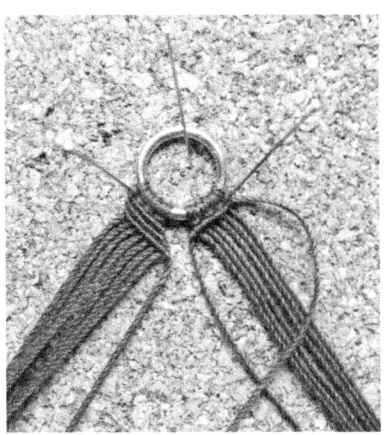

Step 6: At the third-row end, tie around the strand on the right side with the strand closest to the middle on the left. The two sides of the work will now join.

Step 7: On the left-hand side, beginning with the two strands that is closer to the middle, tie a double half hitch. With the strand on the left side, tie around the strand on the right side, as given below.

Repeat the same with the other two strands to the left of what you recently tied, then with each pair until you get to the edge.

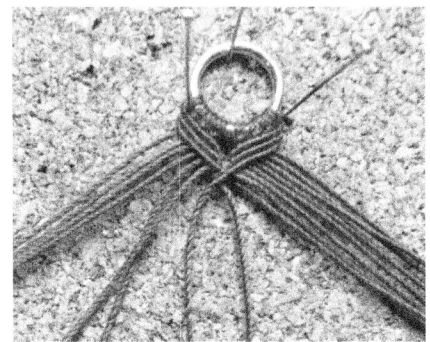

Now, you should have 4 knots as given below

Step 8: Bring the far left strand right through and tie double half hitches just as you did in the first three rows. Place a pin at the sides to keep the work even and when the row has been tied, repeat two more rows as previously done.

Step 9: With the two strands, tie a double half hitch on the right side that is closer to the middle. Repeat the same with the other three pairs. When all the 4 pairs are tied, you should have something shown below.

Step 10: Place a pin at the sides and then make three rows of double half hitch.

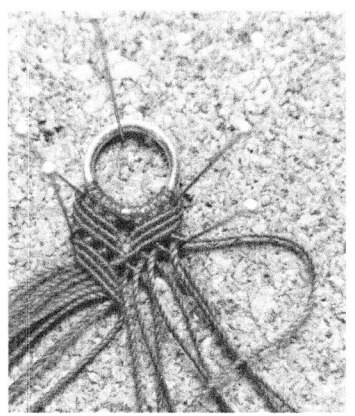

Step 11: At the third row's end, tie around the middle right strand with the middle left strand to connect the sides.

Step 12: Repeat this pattern – one row of paired double half hitches, three rows of standard, and then join at the middle – until you are a large ring short of the desired length. A row of the paired half hitches should be made.

Step 13: Bring the strand on the left side across then tie around it. Don't let it reconnect the remaining strands. Bring the next strand right through and tie around it with all the strands, excluding the first.

Step 14: Tie around each strand until you have just a strand that does the tying. With this, the left side is completed.

Step 15: Repeat the same the right, i.e., one row of paired double half hitches, bringing the strand on the right side across, then knotting around it. Each strand should be tied around without allowing it to reconnect the other strands until you are left with a strand on this side.

Step 16: Add the ring by flipping the work vertically, then slide the two far-left strands right across the ring.

Step 17: Bring the strands around, tying a square knot with the two strands. Ensure the ring is tight to the double half hitch rows.

Step 18: Bring the other strand right across, then bring the fourth strand across the ring, tying a square knot with this pair of strands. Repeat with

each pair of strands until they are all tied. The front should look like this below.

Step 19: A row of double half hitches should be tied on the left. Pull the strands to the middle to prevent them from hanging over the edge and showing on the front. Allow the left strands to join the right strand, then tie a row of double half hitches on the right. One more should be repeated on the left and on the right side row.

When it looks like what is shown below, a coat of fray check or clear fabric glue should be applied to the two rows of knots. Allow it to dry completely. Trim any excess crochet thread carefully.

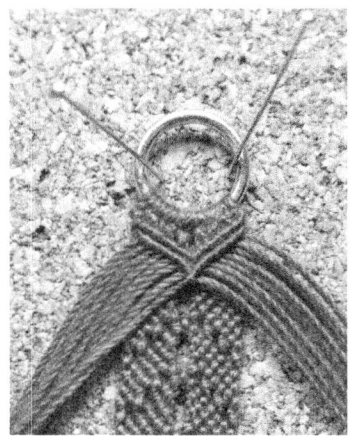

This is the back and front finished

Step 20: Add a clasp, and it is ready to wear

Dyed Macramé Necklace

Not too long ago, I tried out a fancy macramé design called the dyed Macramé necklace and I was pleased with the result. Actually, it was my first time making a macramé dyed necklace. And I absolutely loved how it turned out.

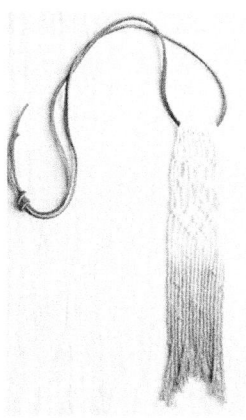

Follow the instructions below to make one for yourself.

What you will need

- Leather lace (long enough to tie around your head)
- Cotton string
- Fabric dye

Instructions

Step 1: Cut a 3 ft long, 8 pieces of cotton string

Step 2: Each string should be folded into half, then tie it to the leather lace using lark's head knot. Tape the untied leather across a table to prevent the top of your necklace from moving around.

Step 3: Make a square knot in sets of four with the 16 strings hanging down. To make a square knot, the first four strings on the left should be taken across string 1, then over string 2 and 3, beneath string 4. Then take string 4 and wrap it beneath string 1 on the right. Continue right under string 2 and 3 then over string 1 on the left.

Step 4: From the last activity in step 3, tighten to the top. Then take string 1 (now on the left) over string 2 and 3, beneath string 4. Take string 4 and wrap it beneath string 1 on the left. Continue this beneath 2 and 3, branching over string 1 on the right side. Tighten to the top as earlier done.

Step 5: For the knots on the top, alternating square knots were used. A square knot for strings 1-4, 5-8, 9-12, 13-16 for row one, strings 3-6 and 11-14 for row two, strings 1-4, 5-8, 9-12,13-16 for row three, strings 3-6 7-10, 11-14 for row four, strings 5-8 and 9-12 for row five, and strings 7-10 for row six.

Then a few random knots were tied on the remaining strings hanging and the bottom trimmed.

Step 6: The leather lace should be tied such that your head fits in it when it is worn.

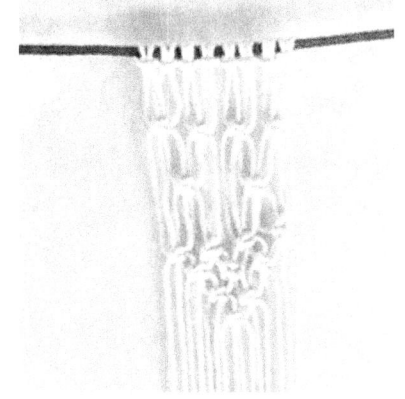

Step 7: For the dye, RIT box dye was used. Just follow the RIT stovetop instructions on how to heat the water and dye.

Step 8: Dip the necklace into the water as high as you want the dye to go up the necklace, then pull it out just a bit, tying it to the handle of the pot to soak for sometime. Continue pulling it up for every 5 -10 minutes for a slight ombre look to be formed.

Rinse it out and allow it to dry.

Easy Macramé Earrings

With a few simple materials, you can make a boho-chic pair of macramé earrings that will surely appear as though they came from a boutique.

Go through the instructions to make a basic pair and a pair that is a bit more intricate.

What you will need

- Wire or cat/ eyelash stiff-bristle comb
- Cotton macramé cord
- Hoop earrings
- Fish hook earring backs (optional)
- Jump rings (optional)
- Scissors
- Jewelry pliers (optional)

Instructions for the first pair

This first type of macramé earring is perfect for beginners because it makes use of one lark's head knot.

Step 1: Place your hoop earring on a leveled surface, then cut a 4-inch length of macramé cord. Fold this cord into half and loop it under your earring hoop.

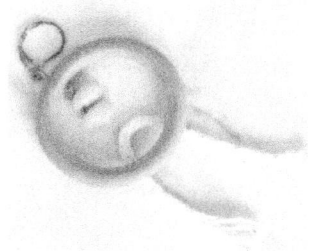

Step 2: Bring the loop of the cord across the earring hoop, tucking the ends via the loop. Pull taut to ensure the cord is firm around the earring hoop.

Repeat this process with extra macramé cords and fill the lower third of the hoop with a lark's head knot.

Step 3: Trim the ends of the cord to an equal length. Then separate the twisted strands of the cords until the ends become frayed. Trim again once frayed, and ensure it is neat and even.

Place your wire comb and gently brush all the fibers for a finished, neat look.

Step 4: Repeat this process with the second hoop earring, and in no time, you will have made a pretty set of macramé earrings you can wear.

Instructions for the second pair

This macramé design does not require a hoop earring. A fishtail earring back and some jump rings is all you need to have this design worn when completed.

Step 1: To begin, cut three pieces of your cotton macramé cord. A piece should be 12-inch and the other two pieces, 6-inch. Fold the 12-inch cord piece into half, bringing the loop to the top. Fold one of the 6-inch cord piece into half, tucking the loop beneath the top of the 12-inch piece, from right to left.

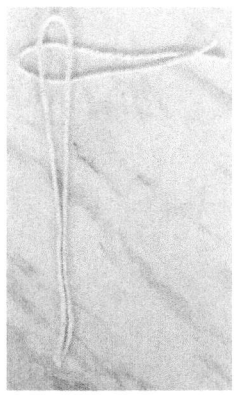

Step 2: Fold the second 6-inch cord into half and tuck this loop up across the first 6-inch cord loop, from left to right.

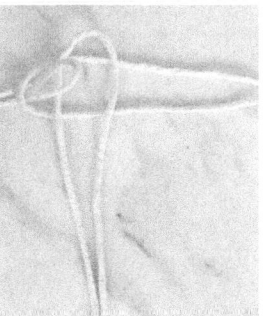

Step 3: Pull the second 6-inch cord through the middle of the 12-inch cord, inserting the ends of the first 6-inch cord across this loop.

Pull both sides of the cords to tighten the knot.

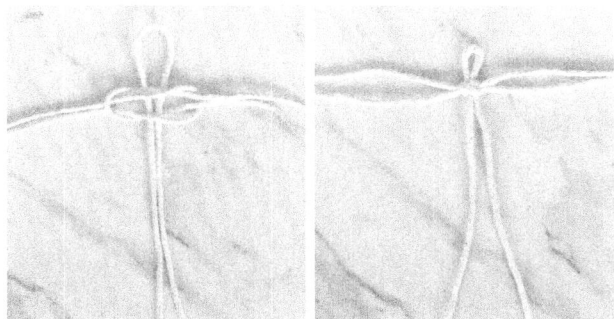

Step 4: Repeat the steps of adding extra two 6-inch loops and tying this knot, but this time, alternate the sides where the first loop was inserted – insert the first loop beneath the middle cord from the left while the second should be from the right. Then start again, this time from the right. Do this continuously until there are ten knots.

Trim the ends into a leaf shape.

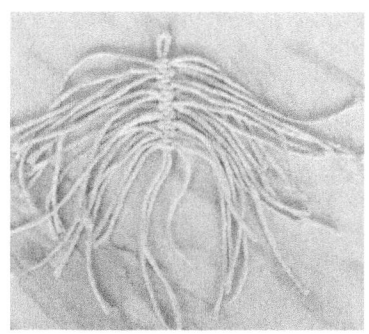 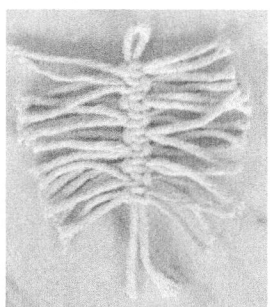

Step 5: Fray and separate the strands of the cords using your fingers and the wire comb. Brush gently using the comb.

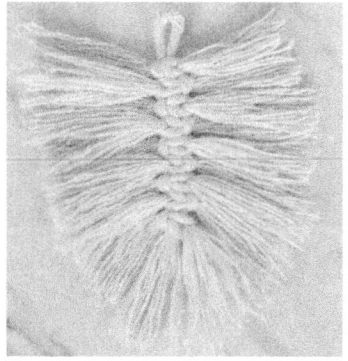

Step 6: Trim again to make a leaf shape then brush with a comb. Add the jump ring to the top loop of the macramé cord.

The end... almost!

Hey! We've made it to the final chapter of this book, and I hope you've enjoyed it so far.

If you have not done so yet, I would be incredibly thankful if you could take just a minute to leave a quick review on Amazon

Reviews are not easy to come by, and as an independent author with a little marketing budget, I rely on you, my readers, to leave a short review on Amazon.

Even if it is just a sentence or two!

So if you really enjoyed this book, please...

\>\> Type this address https://amzn.to/3kdAcxX into your browser to leave a brief review on Amazon.

I truly appreciate your effort to leave your review, as it truly makes a huge difference.

Chapter 7

Frequently Asked Questions (FAQs)

Where can macramé ropes be gotten from?

For beginners, we advise that they start by making use of cotton ropes. Cotton helps the knotting process to be easier and less stressful. There are several cotton manufacturing and distributing companies you can get your cotton supplies from. We recommend that you purchase 100% certified cotton. This is the same quality and texture of cotton used for children's clothing. They are not produced with chemicals and they give the best experience while making macramé designs.

What is the difference between a rope and a cord?

The two words are used interchangeably but in reality, there is no much difference between the two. A cord is used to include other materials like ropes and strands while a rope has a single meaning or significance. A cord can be twisted, braided, or woven. Ropes are grouped under a cord and consist of a number of fibers, twisted, braided, or woven. Standard measures of ropes include 5mm, 3 mm, and 3-ply twisted ropes.

What quantity of rope should I use for a project?

This will depend on the type of knot and pattern you wish to achieve. When making a loose net, your measurement should be four times the length of the piece. If, for example, you need a project 3ft long, then you will need a 12mm rope. If the project you want to create entails lots of detailed knots with little spaces, you should take your measurement 6 times the original length.

As a beginner, it is not healthy running out of ropes. You should have a plan on the type of design and project you want to embark on. The more you practice measurements made on estimated project length, you will get better at predicting the length of rope to use. You would even with clear precision know what length to use on mere sight.

What type of rope should I use?

There are a variety of ropes and cords to be used for macramé projects, which include cotton, acrylic, nylon and twine materials. Cotton ropes are commonly used, except you have special projects that need other materials. There are two types of cotton ropes: braided and twisted ropes. Braided ropes are composed of six strands of cotton, braided to form a single rope.

What knot do I begin from?

When learning to do projects with macramé, it is advisable to start simple and gradually work your way up to complex designs. The square knot is a good start for beginners. Another alternative to this is the alternating square knot. The difference between both is the procedures used in knotting. It is the most basic knot you can apply for a number of projects.

How do you maintain tension?

To achieve this, you need to understand the place of consistency in practice. The way you tighten your knots will determine the size of the knot. If you don't maintain the same consistency, you will end up with an irregular knot size. As you practice over time, you will be more adjusted to the right size of knots throughout your project. At the early stages, some of the knots you'll make will need to be loosened and so it is good that you don't tighten them so much.

Why do I need leftover ropes?

As a learner, never get tired of failing with your macramé designs. For many, the biggest challenge you'll need to overcome is being precise with the amount of rope you cut. As it has been stated earlier, the length of rope to use depends on the type of knot and length of the project you want to create. Another thing that affects the rope length is the tension applied to each knot. Having excesses in rope length is far better than having shortages of ropes when you've already begun crafting your design. There is a couple of other projects that can be carried out using your leftover ropes. Examples of such include macramé leaves, key chains or bookmarks. You can add them as fringes to your projects.

What is the difference between macramé and crochets?

This is another key area of confusion for many. Though they may seem similar, they are not the same. Both of them are textile crafts and share similar techniques. Macramé makes use of knots, hitches and weaves to create patterns and designs. Crotchets, on the other hand, makes use of needles and yarn loops to make designs. Crotchets are more commonly used in clothing designs, while macramé find a vast application for interior decorations.

How can I make macramé a full-time profession?

As with other handcrafts, macramé can be made on a professional level as a lot of profit can be generated from it. The good part of it all is that macramé can be created by anyone who decides to take an interest in it. To become a professional at macramé, you need to invest a good amount of time in practice. Familiarize yourself with all the basic knots as much as possible and learn to do simple projects like bracelets, key chains, and plant hangers, among others.

Printed in Great Britain
by Amazon